Praying In The Presence Of
Our Lord

WITH
St. Thomas
Aquinas

D1371644

Praying In The Presence Of
Our Lord

WITH
ST. THOMAS AQUINAS

MIKE AQUILINA

FR. BENEDICT J. GROESCHEL, C.F.R.
SERIES EDITOR

Our Sunday Visitor Publishing Division
Our Sunday Visitor, Inc.
Huntington, Indiana 46750

Nihil Obstat:
Rev. Kris D. Stubna, S.T.D.
Censor Librorum

Imprimatur:
✠ Donald William Wuerl
Bishop of Pittsburgh
August 2, 2001

The *Nihil Obstat* and the *Imprimatur* are declarations that a work is considered to be free from doctrinal or moral error. It is not implied that those who have granted the same agree with the contents, opinions, or statements expressed.

Scripture citations, unless otherwise noted, are from the *Revised Standard Version, Catholic Edition* (RSV), copyright © 1965 and 1966 by the Division of Christian Education of the National Council of Churches of Christ in the U.S.A., and are used by permission of the copyright owner.

Every reasonable effort has been made to determine copyright holders and to secure permissions as needed. If any copyrighted materials have been inadvertently used without proper credit being given in one manner or another, please notify Our Sunday Visitor in writing so that future editions may be corrected accordingly.

Our Sunday Visitor Publishing Division
Our Sunday Visitor, Inc.
200 Noll Plaza
Huntington, IN 46750

ISBN: 0-87973-958-4
LCCCN: 2001135260

Cover design by Tyler Ottinger
Cover art by Robert F. McGovern
Interior design by Sherri L. Hoffman

PRINTED IN THE UNITED STATES OF AMERICA

✠

_____

*Dedicated to the memory
of Robert E. Tschan, my friend and teacher*

Contents

✠

___

Introduction

✠

$\mathcal{T}$his book is so beautiful that I wish I had written it myself. It may seem to many readers a bit odd to write a book about praying with ancient Latin hymns, even if they are translated into English. How can you pray with ancient hymns? I'll tell you about my experience with these Latin hymns, and so will our author, Mike Aquilina, who has been doing the same thing himself. It is very pleasant to learn to pray with poetry. Believe me — learn to pray in the presence of Christ with St. Thomas's hymns and you will never pray the same again.

Praying with poetry is all about beauty, and it is not easy to write about beauty in our ugly times. We live with ugly art, ugly buildings, and even ugly churches. We listen to ugly music and ugly sounds. Modern art galleries are filled with ugly objects, even absolutely hideous ones. Some virus infected Western civilization in the mid-twentieth century and caused a preoccupation with the ugly, the discordant, and the cynical. Ours is a culture of death, one without values, heroes, ideas, or beauty. But beauty is one of the transcendent qualities of being, of God himself, and so beauty and the desire for beauty do not go away. When St. Augustine prayed to God, he cried: "O Beauty, so ancient and yet so new, too late have I known you, too late have I loved you."

Let me give you an example of how beauty comes back even after it has been purposely banished. Some years ago, I received a pleasant surprise when reading *The New York Times Book Review*, which is usually filled with ugly books. I was about to pass over an essay by a very capable Jewish writer, Leon Edel, who was writing about Edith Wharton, a rich lady who celebrated New York's Protestant upper class a century ago. (I'm not the Edith Wharton type.) Suddenly I saw the words *Corpus Christi* in the middle of the article. Edel went on to describe how every year Mrs. Wharton opened the magnificent garden of her château outside Paris to the local parish for the feast of Corpus Christi — *la fête-Dieu*. He even described the procession of the Blessed Sacrament in the monstrance and the children singing and spreading rose petals along the garden path. The essay brought back beautiful memories of my own youth and the solemn singing of the great eucharistic hymns, the very ones that are in this book. Why did a Jewish writer recall this procession sixty years later in a very secular newspaper? For only one reason — because it was beautiful.

Mike Aquilina has captured and explained, as far as beautiful things can be explained, the profound eucharistic theology of St. Thomas. This great intellect, St. Thomas, whose writings are never dull but can be daunting, wrote with personal devotion of the mystery of the Holy Eucharist in magnificent poetry.

Just a generation before St. Thomas St. Francis popularized eucharistic worship and established the requirements for reverence to the presence of Christ in his three circular letters, which went to all the clergy, to all governors and rulers, and to all friars. This insistence on reverence for the person of Christ in the Eucharist characterized St. Francis, St. Dominic, and their first friars, and became a powerful expression in the works of St. Thomas. When he was asked by Pope Urban IV to write a whole liturgical celebration for the new feast of Corpus Christi, St. Thomas composed the feast's Mass and Office, which have been called the literary masterpieces of the Catholic liturgy. Unfortunately, these works have been somewhat dismembered in recent years. I pray that they will all be restored, and I hope that this book will be part of the process of restoration.

Having meditated on these hymns for years, let me offer you a few hints, which fit in perfectly with what my friend Mike has written. Poetry is a matter of the music of spoken words. You have to taste the words. Mike uses elegant translations of the Latin that were written in what is now called the golden age of English literature. However, savoring the words is only the beginning. You must move on to the profound scriptural and theological meaning of the words.

Perhaps a theological insight may be helpful here. St. Thomas wrote immediately after a time when some theologians tried to reduce the Eucharist to a mere symbol. Basing his writings on the most ancient Church Fathers and the tradition coming from St. Paul's own words in 1 Corinthians 11, St. Thomas maintained that Jesus Christ is truly and really present.

Although he used several arguments, one is really meaningful to those who already know Christ's Real Presence from personal and prayerful experience. Pointing out that the sacrifices of the Old Testament were, in fact, symbols of the coming sacrifice of the Messiah, St. Thomas maintains that the Eucharist is something more. The following quotation, taken from Father Aidan Nichols, a greatly respected Dominican theologian, summarizes St. Thomas's teaching:

> Appropriately, it contains Christ himself who suffered for us, and that not merely in a token (*significatio*) but in actual reality as well. Secondly, such a real presence, Thomas argues, better befits the charity of Christ which led him to take a human body for our sakes at the Incarnation. It is in the highest degree proper to friendship, Thomas explains, that friends should live together. They should share that common life which bodily communication makes possible. In heaven, we shall see Christ, the King, in his beauty; but even here on our pilgrimage, he has not left us without his bodily presence. So Thomas calls this sacrament since it joins Christ and ourselves so intimately, *signum maximae caritatis,* 'the sign of the greatest possible charity,' and *nostrae spei sublevamentum,* the 'arousal of our hope.'[1]

[1] *The Holy Eucharist: From the New Testament to Pope John Paul II* (Dublin: Veritas, 1991), 67–68.

St. Thomas also points out that in the Eucharist, Christ is present in His humanity — His manhood — as well as His divinity. In fact, His divinity makes Him present everywhere, but in the Eucharist He is present in His humanity, in His Body and Blood. He is present as Son of God and Son of Mary.

Keeping this theology in mind (and when you pray regularly before the Eucharist, it becomes second nature), you can move easily to the original Latin words. This is not a difficult transition even if you are not familiar with Latin. Let me give you an example. Those who love opera love a particular work in its original language even if they are not fluent in that language. Think of "Ridi, Pagliaccio" from "Vesti la Giubba," or even "O Sole Mio" or "Santa Lucia." Anyone familiar with these great songs will know the significance of these phrases without knowing what every word means. The very moving "Ridi, Pagliaccio," sung by the broken-hearted clown, always brings a moment of sorrow to me when I hear it.

We can have the same experience with the phrases of Latin prayers, but on a much deeper level. Most of my readers will experience a prayerful moment listening to the words *Ave Maria* and recalling Gounod's beautiful music. This experience will bring Gounod's arrangement back to mind. Older readers can do the same thing with the "Kyrie Eleison" and the "Pater Noster" and especially the "Gloria in Excelsis Deo." Those who enjoyed an integrated Catholic education in the past will come to life with the words *Pange Lingua Gloriosi* even without knowing the precise meaning of each word. The same is true of *O Salutaris Hostia* and *Tantum Ergo*. Even words not understood can communicate many things by the context in which they have been previously experienced, especially if they are sung. Modern urban congregations can relate to the folk hymns of Latin American and Caribbean traditions. We sing words like the solemn Latin American folk hymn "*Resucito*," or the Caribbean "*Kumbaya*," without knowing that these words mean "he is risen" and "O Lord, be with me." As we study our Latin hymns, we must bear in mind that unknown words with music take on a meaning by reason of their context.

Now we are ready to move to the highest level of experienced words by studying the Latin hymns of the great Angelic Doctor, St. Thomas. First, it is important to know what he means by the words. Consider the first hymn that Mike analyzes, "Lauda, Sion." We have all seen the word Zion. Sometimes it has strong political or even military significance. But what does it mean biblically and spiritually? After you read Mike's excellent commentary, you will be enriched with a totally new understanding. Sion or Zion will never again mean the same thing to you. For instance, "Lauda, Sion" will take on a very special meaning for anyone who has participated in the eucharistic procession and blessing of the sick at Lourdes. Thousands of voices are raised in the candlelight procession, and the meaning of the words *Lauda, Sion*, "Zion, praise your Savior," will fill your soul. You can hear the whole Church singing. It is the new Zion, the everlasting Church of the heavenly Jerusalem, the eternal procession of the saints. With this understanding of words and music you are ready for a great feast of meaning and prayer.

For many reasons — I suspect most of them growing out of centuries of persecution and disparagement by the so-called enlightened — Christianity has become impoverished. For more than a century the popes have struggled against this impoverishment. In the English-speaking world it seems to be true that the more affluent Catholics become, the poorer they seem to become culturally. The smaller number of Catholics who live in poverty seem to be mysteriously preserved by God himself from this general intimidation. The rest of us are culturally and intellectually poorer than we were fifty years ago. Catholic education, which did a great job of assimilating the immigrants and their children, has somehow in recent decades sold out to the banalities of secular culture or anti-culture.

This is a shame. We lose much. Sixty years ago a very bright Harvard student from a well-known Protestant family was deeply impressed when he went into a typical working-class Catholic church and heard the people singing the Latin hymns of St. Thomas Aquinas. I was there when the Holy Father put the red hat on this man, Cardinal Avery Dulles. The great Jesuit poet Gerard Manley Hopkins reminds us that the Holy Spirit broods over our dark world with bright wings. The unexpected and frequently opposed revival of devotion to Christ in the Eucharist, which

James Monti and I described in our book *In the Presence of Our Lord,* is an opportunity for the revival of a significant aspect of Catholic culture and spirituality. Eucharistic adoration is the Catholic devotion *par excellence.* Mike Aquilina will help you with one of the most personally enriching aspects of this devotion, the hymns of St. Thomas. Pray with St. Thomas and you will be part of an exciting new Catholic revival — a spiritual revival, but a cultural one as well.

FATHER BENEDICT J. GROESCHEL, C.F.R.
Trinity Retreat House
Larchmont, New York
January 28, 2002
Feast of St. Thomas Aquinas

About This Book . . .

✠

This book presents the poems of St. Thomas in their original Latin alongside the English translations I found to be most pleasing and accurate. For each poem, I wrote seven meditations that examine selected words, phrases, or lines in light of the theological works of St. Thomas, especially the *Summa Theologica*, as well as the early biographies of St. Thomas, which were compiled for his canonization inquiry. In some cases, the meditations are mostly paraphrased lines gathered from throughout the *Summa*. Unless otherwise noted, quotations attributed to St. Thomas are taken from the *Summa*; biographical details about St. Thomas are taken from the earliest lives of the saint, including those submitted for the process of canonization. A list of reference sources is included at the end of this book.

I composed these meditations to help readers pray the prayers of the saint as he prayed them. For the best results, we should pray them, as Thomas did, in the presence of Our Lord. Pray to Jesus, whenever you can, before his tabernacle, where he dwells among us.

"To come to Jesus is to believe in him," St. Thomas wrote. "For we draw near to God not by the steps the body takes, but by those the mind takes. And the first step toward God is faith."

Preface

✠

Who is poet laureate of heaven?

Even the most self-sure literary critic would have trouble making that call. Consider the poets we know to be in glory, the canonized saints: Francis of Assisi, John of the Cross, Bernard of Clairvaux. . . . Give Dante the benefit of the doubt, and the competition gets pretty tough.

But if God were to permit a vote, with all the Catholic faithful as electors, the results would surely show a landslide.

No poet could surpass St. Thomas Aquinas.

Indeed, except for King David, no poet in history — not Homer, not Virgil — has had quite St. Thomas's appeal in the West. Over the last seven centuries, many millions of us have grown up singing his lyrics at Benediction and Holy Communion: *Tantum ergo Sacramentum veneremur cernui . . . O salutaris Hostia, quae caeli pandis ostium . . . Panis angelicus fit panis hominum!* In Latin or English, these are among the most memorable hymns of our faith — and, in spite of their peculiarly Catholic themes (all expound the doctrine of transubstantiation), they have proved powerfully appealing to Protestant believers, too.

What explains the appeal of St. Thomas's poetry? Certainly not his name. Everyone knows that St. Thomas wrote the *Summa Theologica*. Few people know he wrote the "Panis Angelicus."

Neither can we credit Thomas's reputation as a poet to the quantity of his production. He probably wrote only five poems in his life:"Lauda, Sion,""Pange, Lingua" (with "Tantum Ergo"),"Verbum Supernum" (with "O Salutaris Hostia"),"Sacris Solemniis" (with "Panis Angelicus"), and "Adoro Te Devote." Just 188 lines — minuscule compared to the output of a Robert Frost or Emily Dickinson.

But meditate on those lines — for their religious depth, their aesthetic value, or their doctrinal clarity — and you'll find treasures. If you know a smattering of Latin, you'll discover the masterpiece that inspired Cesar Franck to compose his greatest work when he set the "Panis Angelicus" to music. You'll recognize also the original genius behind Gerard Manley Hopkins's poem "Godhead Here in Hiding." And you'll know why St. Thomas has appealed, however anonymously, to the great congregations of believers through the centuries. Not just to the scholarly or the refined, but (to steal one of his own lines) to *pauper, servus, et humilis* — to the poor, the servant, the lowly.

The Charity of the Poet

Only such a poet, and such a saint, could satisfy the tastes of so many millions of God's people. We learn from his earliest biographers that Friar Thomas was an adviser to the king of France, yet his homilies made unlettered peasants weep. This charity, this love for others regardless of their station, enabled Thomas to see what was universally beautiful in poetry. There is in the "Pange, Lingua" none of the intricacy of the court poetry of his age; but today the court poems are forgotten by all but a handful of medievalists. Neither, however, is there the coarseness of folk rhymes or the sentimentality of "inspirational verse." Those qualities, he knew, make for ephemera.

As in his philosophy, so in his lyrics: St. Thomas got to the essence of the thing. He composed poems that are pure poetry.

This fact always comes as a shock to people who have tried without success to wade through his philosophy or theology. The *Summa* is no wading pool; it's a great sea, traveled safely and surely only by trained navigators. The specialized vocabulary makes difficult reading. The unrelenting, unpicturesque prose was written for minds disciplined as most of ours are not.

But Thomas's poems wash over us like waves: The great sea now comes to us on shore. Even if we hear the lyrics sung in Latin — even if we know no Latin — we recognize that these are works that glorify God. The sound itself makes a petition. Rhyme brings perfect closure to lines and verses; vigorous rhythms set a new pace for our hearts; syllables echo hypnotically from line to line. And in those waves of unfamiliar words, we glimpse the familiar: *gloriosi, mysterium, pretiosi* — glorious, mystery, precious.

The timing couldn't be more perfect. Since we usually hear St. Thomas's hymns during eucharistic adoration, his words suggest themselves to us, join our own words in prayer, and bring our own devotion closer to the devotion of the saints.

More Than Meets the Ear

But, to know these poems best, we need to study their sense as well as their sound. The two elements are inseparable in great poems. Sound suggests sense: Chesterton compares the opening words of the "Pange, Lingua" to a cymbal crash. And sense prepares us for the inevitable sound, perfectly placed and timed: in "Lauda, Sion" and "Sacris Solemniis," when Thomas speaks of the completion of the old dispensation, he places the words *terminum* and *terminat* — "end" — at the lines' end, achieving a beautiful, unmistakable sense of finality.

Much of this elegance, unfortunately, is lost in translation. Translators often must choose to sacrifice one element, sound or sense, for the sake of another. In Latin, a line could be both precise and artful, while in English its verbatim rendering may make it clumsy.

Still, translations will reach most readers as Latin can not. So in this book I have provided English translations together with the Latin originals. In the meditations, I have sometimes drawn from several translations, from the hands of different authors. I urge you, however, to spend time with the originals. You'll draw closer to the mystery of the charity of the poet, and, perhaps, closer to the mystery of St. Thomas's subject: charity himself.

Poet By Decree

The story of St. Thomas's angelic hymns begins with a heavenly vision. In the mid-thirteenth century, in

Mont Cornillon, Belgium, lived a Cistercian nun named Juliana, who was especially devoted to the Blessed Sacrament. Once, while praying, she saw a vision of a full moon, radiant but for one black spot. Later, in a dream, Our Lord appeared to her and explained the figures: The moon was his Church, which would be incomplete (thus the black spot) as long as it marked no feast in honor of the sacrament of his body. Juliana reported the vision to her superiors, and eventually the story made its way to her bishop, who ordered the feast to be observed locally.

Surely it wasn't long before the city of Paris knew of Juliana. And of all the people in Paris the Dominican community, where St. Thomas lived and worked, would be most moved by the revelation. Since the days of St. Dominic, eucharistic devotion had been central to the life of the Order of Preachers.

Shortly after Juliana's death in 1258, a priest from her diocese was elected pope. As Urban IV, this man would become St. Thomas's great patron. At Urban's command, Thomas produced volumes of theology, controversy, and Scripture study, work that earned him the title "Angelic Doctor."

According to some biographers, the pope was so pleased with Thomas that he twice offered the friar a cardinal's hat. The second time took place after Urban had read a section of the *Catena Aurea*, Thomas's "golden chain" that traced Christian doctrines through the Scripture commentaries of the most ancient Fathers of the Church. Filled with gratitude and awe, the pontiff wanted to repay his theologian. But, again,

Thomas refused the red hat. The pope offered anything else — anything within his power.

And today, across these many centuries, we can imagine Thomas's smile as he chose his reward: He asked the pope to fulfill Juliana's vision. He would have a feast in honor of the Blessed Sacrament.

Urban granted Thomas's wish, but showed that he could be just as demanding. If the Church would have the feast of Christ's body, she would pray on that day using Thomas's words. Urban's philosopher would turn poet to compose the Mass and Office for Corpus Christi.

Now, this request was, on the surface, absurd. The Jesuit scholar Martin D'Arcy wrote: "We should never have guessed from the prose works that St. Thomas had any poetical gifts. One looks in vain for purple passages, for picturesque phrases, for sudden and original epithets and images. His style seems in fact at first reading, just dull, good jog-trot prose. . . . And yet in the Office of Corpus Christi he composed a perfect work of literature."

G. K Chesterton, too, marveled at the pope's strange choice of Thomas as a poet. Thomas, he said, "was an eminently practical prose writer; some would say a very prosaic prose writer. He maintained controversy with an eye on only two qualities: clarity and courtesy." Not cleverness, not artfulness. Urban's choice was truly folly to the gentiles.

But we can see it also as proof positive of the authority of God's vicar on earth. After all, it worked. Chesterton goes on to say that the "composer of the

Corpus Christi service was not merely what even the wild and woolly would call a poet; he was what the most fastidious would call an artist."

Yes, St. Thomas, the same man who wrote, in *On Being and Essence*, "Since that which has the nature of a genus, species, or difference is predicated of this particular designated thing, the essence, expressed as a part . . . cannot possibly have the nature of a universal, that is, of a genus or species," also wrote, in the first vespers hymn for Corpus Christi:

> *Hail angelic bread of heaven,*
> *Now become the pilgrim's leaven,*
> *Bread of life to children given,*
> *That to dogs must not be thrown,*
> *Through prophetic signs narrated,*
> *Once as Isaac immolated,*
> *By the Paschal Lamb predated,*
> *In the olden manna known . . .*
>
> *Thou who all things canst and knowest,*
> *Who thyself as food bestowest,*
> *Make us, where thy face thou showest,*
> *With thy saints, though least and lowest,*
> *Guests and fellow heirs to be.*

Still, though Thomas had the skill, one might question whether poetry was the best use of his time. He was, after all, the most brilliant and prestigious theologian of his time, and he was working on perhaps the most important theological project in history. Yet, as A.G. Sertillanges, O.P., noted: "He believed that this was not a distraction, but another means of teaching the truth. . . . As this sacrament is for all, so his hymns are for all, whereas his abstract writings, in themselves at least, are meant for a few."

Thomas's lively verses are almost enough to make us believe an old legend about St. Thomas, of dubious historical value.

The story goes that Pope Urban actually set up a competition for the writing of the Corpus Christi Mass and Office. The contestants were two: St. Thomas and the Franciscan luminary St. Bonaventure. Both men were ordered to prepare their prayers and hymns, then "face off," reading their work before judges.

On the appointed day, Thomas read first, and as he pronounced the last, profound verses of the matins hymn — the "Panis Angelicus" — Friar Bonaventure began to weep. Bystanders heard the crumbling of parchment and saw Bonaventure's manuscript falling in pieces to the floor. . . .

Today, the true details of the Corpus Christi story are almost indistinguishable among the fancies of hagiography. But one theme is common to all accounts: St. Thomas was a poet made, not born. He was a poet made by decree and, no doubt, by grace.

'Lauda, Sion'

Thomas's grace overflows to us in the "Lauda, Sion," his sequence to be recited or chanted at Mass on Corpus Christi. This is his longest poem by far, and it is insistently formal. Scholars believe that Thomas modeled its rhythms after those of "Laudes Crucis Attollamus" by Adam of St. Victor, a twelfth-century poet. In both poems, the six-line verses alternate two eight-syllable, four-beat lines with one seven-syllable, four-beat line:

> *Lauda, Sion, Salvatorem!*
> *Lauda, ducem et pastorem*
> *In hymnis et canticis:*
> *Quantum potes, tantum aude,*
> *Quia maior omni laude,*
> *Nec laudare sufficis!*

H. T. Henry captured the vigor of Thomas's original by matching both the stress and rhyme schemes, while achieving a near-literal translation.

> *Praise, O Sion, praise thy Savior,*
> *Shepherd, Prince, with glad behavior,*
> *Praise in hymn and canticle:*
> *Sing his glory without measure,*
> *For the merit of your treasure*
> *Never shall your praises fill!*

The eminent Cambridge scholar of medieval poetry F. J. E. Raby called the "Lauda, Sion" "the supreme dogmatic poem of the Middle Ages," noting that Thomas's "doctrinal exposition follows closely" the sequence of arguments that deal with the Eucharist in the *Summa Theologica*. Indeed, the vocabulary, too, is identical. Raby explained that the "Lauda, Sion" "never wanders from the correct scholastic terminology. . . . [T]he thought is hard and closely woven."

Yet the diction in the poem is far different, far more lyrical. "It is a poem as well as a dogmatic exposition," said Raby. "The verses have an austerity and grandeur which no Latin poet of the Middle Ages ever equaled."

There are dozens of English translations of the "Lauda, Sion," including those made by the major British poets Robert Southwell and Richard Crashaw. It appears in many Protestant hymnals, including those of Lutheran and Episcopal churches in America. The Calvinist historian Philip Schaff praised it in spite of its bald affirmation of the Real Presence. Martin Luther stands seemingly alone in despising the hymn, charging that Thomas wrote "as though he were the worst enemy of God, or else an idiot."

'Pange, Lingua'

"Pange, Lingua" (the hymn for first vespers) is the Corpus Christi hymn most often sung. For many years, the Church required that the last two verses, beginning with "Tantum Ergo," be sung any time the Blessed Sacrament was exposed. In solemn processions with the sacrament — on Holy Thursday and Corpus Christi, for example — the faithful usually chanted all six verses.

John Mason Neale, the Anglican priest who translated many of the devotional poems of the ancient Church, praised the "Pange, Lingua" as one of the greatest hymns in the West, second only to the "Dies Irae."

Professor Raby, too, considered this hymn "beyond all praise, for its severe and rigid beauty, its precision of thought. . . . [T]he 'Pange, Lingua'," he concluded, "is one of the most sublime productions of sacred poetry."

Listen and you'll know why:

Pange, lingua, gloriosi
Corporis mysterium
Sanguinisque pretiosi
Quem in mundi pretium
Fructus ventris generosi
Rex effudit gentium.

No English translation has come near the mellifluous quality of the original. No English translation is as concise and powerful as this first evensong. "Sing, my tongue, the mystery of the glorious body, and of the precious blood which the King of Nations, fruit of a noble womb, poured out as the world's ransom."

Thomas returns to a theme he introduced in "Lauda, Sion." He develops the notion of the Last Supper fulfilling everything in the old dispensation — the Law and the types.

He ends by praising the mysteries, by falling "down in adoration" of Trinity and sacrament. In a profoundly moving line, Thomas — the philosopher who was the senses' greatest champion — invokes faith, "where the feeble senses fail."

Thomas built on strong foundations when he composed the "Pange, Lingua." He takes his opening line from a sixth-century hymn of Venantius Fortunatus, "*Pange, lingua, gloriosi proelium certaminis*" ("Sing, my tongue, the glorious battle"), on the triumph of the cross. Thomas, however, showed himself to be at the avant-garde of his craft and followed the currents of thirteenth-century Latin poetry rather than the classical meter of Fortunatus. Thomas's poem is much richer in rhyme as well. Many years later, when Pope Urban VIII declared that all Latin hymns should be revised to return to the classical forms, he made an exception for Thomas's hymns, which he ordered not to be touched.

There are more than thirty English translations of this hymn, which H.T. Henry called "magically beautiful." Though the chant setting is familiar to most Catholics, the "Pange, Lingua" has also lent itself to many standard hymn arrangements — and at least one critically acclaimed jazz interpretation, by pianist Dave Brubeck, a convert to the Catholic faith.

'Verbum Supernum'

This hymn, for the hour of lauds, is used almost as widely as the "Pange, Lingua." Its concluding verses, beginning with "O Salutaris Hostia," appear in the customary rite of Benediction and Exposition of the Blessed Sacrament. Father Edward Caswall's translation has been the preferred version of missal publishers for more than a century:

> O saving Victim, opening wide
> The gate of heaven to man below,
> Our foes press on from every side;
> Thine aid supply, thy strength bestow.

"Verbum Supernum" is a poetic exploration of the dogmas of the Trinity, the Incarnation, and the

Eucharist. St. Thomas demonstrates that these three mysteries are interrelated and, indeed, inseparable in the mind and heart of the faithful Christian.

In writing this hymn, St. Thomas built upon a fourth- or fifth-century Advent hymn, often attributed to St. Ambrose of Milan, which contains the same opening line. Some scholars believe he also drew from a hymn written by a Cistercian monk, John, when Corpus Christi was still only a local feast in Belgium. In any event, Thomas is usually credited at least with artful editorial work.

In this hymn, again, Thomas develops his favorite themes: the fulfillment of Old Testament types, the pivotal event of the Last Supper, and the price of our redemption. He closes with praise for the Trinity and a prayer for heaven.

'Sacris Solemniis'

This hymn, for the hour of matins, is St. Thomas's least doctrinal hymn, but the most evocative. One critic compares it to Leonardo da Vinci's "Last Supper." Thomas takes us to the upper room and seats us at Christ's Passover table. The poet describes Our Lord's actions — the preparation of the food, the breaking of the bread, his words of blessing. The poem is suffused with warmth; Thomas describes the events in terms of deep friendship and human emotion.

In the next-to-last verses, Thomas then loses himself in wonder: "The bread of angels becomes man's bread; the bread from heaven puts an end to the foreshadowing. What a marvelous thing this is! The pauper, the slave, the lowly feeds upon his Lord!"

In hymnals, the last two verses often stand on their own as the "Panis Angelicus." With Cesar Franck's setting, this melody has become a standard on classical-music programs. Like Schubert's "Ave Maria," it is a Latin hymn familiar even to unbelievers. In the late twentieth century, recordings by the great operatic tenor Luciano Pavarotti brought Franck's "Panis Angelicus" into the homes of millions. Catholic hymnals and missals, however, have tended to favor the simpler, stately setting by Louis Lambilotte. It is more singable, yet nonetheless beautiful.

'Adoro Te Devote'

The "Adoro Te Devote" is unique among the poems attributed to St. Thomas because it is not part of the Church's official prayers for Corpus Christi. In the centuries following Thomas's death, it has been used widely as a prayer of private devotion and an act of thanksgiving after Holy Communion.

In the early twentieth century, scholars tended to doubt that St. Thomas wrote the "Adoro Te Devote," because the earliest surviving manuscripts do not bear his name — indeed, they bear no name at all. The three surviving manuscripts from the fourteenth century, however, all bear the Angelic Doctor's name. Opinion began to change in the mid-twentieth century, following the intensive historical and literary analysis of Professor Raby and others.

Tradition makes a mighty claim for the authenticity of the "Adoro Te." The vocabulary is surely Thomas's. The poetic style, however, is quite different from that of his other poems. Rhythms are looser, more suggestive of meditation.

Some of the early manuscripts claim that Thomas prayed the "Adoro Te" in thanksgiving after his last Communion. This would seem to contradict the testimony of the witnesses at his canonization process — who reported his last prayers in great detail — but it is not beyond possibility.

Dom Eugene Vandeur wrote a splendid book of reflections on the lines of this poem. He sees, in the seven stanzas of the "Adoro Te," the seven stages of the soul on its way to union with its eucharistic God: adoration of God, adherence to God, confession of God, abandonment to God, hunger for God, purification by God, and happiness in God.

The Hidden Poet

Perhaps no one summed up the life of our poet better than Etienne Gilson, who spent his own lifetime studying the work of Thomas the philosopher. "We . . . pass from the philosophy of St. Thomas to his prayer, and from his prayer to his poetry without any sense of change in the order of ideas. For there is no change. His philosophy is as rich in beauty as his poetry is heavy with thought." Gilson goes on to quote the French poet Remy de Gourmont — an esthete and a relativist, whose thought was far from that of St. Thomas; yet he could say that, as poet and as philosopher, "St. Thomas Aquinas is always equal in genius, a genius of force and certitude, of firmness and precision. All he wishes to say, he affirms with such decisiveness of thought that 'doubt, affrighted, flies.' "

Hidden away in the last pages of St. Thomas's voluminous collected works are his poems and hymns. And there is St. Thomas as everyone's companion, not just the scholar's. He's our good teacher, a lively singer, the angelic poet.

The poet laureate of heaven? Just wait and see.

I.

Lauda, Sion

Praise, O Zion

Lauda, Sion

Lauda, Sion, Salvatorem,
Lauda Ducem et Pastorem,
In hymnis et canticis.
Quantum potes, tantum aude:
Quia maior omni laude,
Nec laudare sufficis.

Laudis thema specialis,
Panis vivus et vitalis
Hodie proponitur.
Quem in sacrae mensae coenae,
Turbae fratrum duodenae
Datum non ambigitur.

Sit laus plena, sit sonora,
Sit iucunda, sit decora
Mentis iubilatio.
Namque dies est solemnis
Qua recolitur perennis
Mensae institutio.

In hac mensa novi Regis,
Novum Pascha novae legis,
Phase vetus terminat.
Iam vetustas novitati,
Umbra cedit veritati,
Noctem lux eliminat.

Praise, O Zion

Praise, O Zion, praise thy Savior,
Shepherd, Prince, with glad behavior,
Praise in hymn and canticle:
Sing his glory without measure,
For the merit of your treasure
Never shall your praises fill.

Wondrous theme of mortal singing,
Living bread and bread life-bringing,
Sing we on this joyful day:
At the Lord's own table given
To the twelve as bread from heaven,
Doubting not, we firmly say.

Sing his praise with voice sonorous;
Every heart shall hear the chorus
Swell in melody sublime:
For this day the Shepherd gave us
Flesh and blood to feed and save us,
Lasting to the end of time.

At the new King's sacred table,
The new Law's new Pasch is able
To succeed the ancient rite:
Old to new its place hath given,
Truth has far the shadows driven,
Darkness flees before the light.

Quod in coena Christus gessit,
Faciendum hoc expressit
In sui memoriam.
Docti sacris institutis,
Panem, vinum in salutis
Consecramus hostiam.

Dogma datur Christianis,
Quod in carnem transit panis,
Et vinum in sanguinem.
Quod non capis, quod non vides,
Animosa firmat fides,
Praeter rerum ordinem.

Sub diversis speciebus,
Signis tamen, et non rebus,
Latent res eximiae.
Caro cibus, sanguis potus:
Manet tamen Christus totus
Sub utraque specie.

A sumente non concisus,
Non confractus, non divisus:
Integer accipitur.
Sumit unus, sumunt mille:
Quantum isti, tantum ille:
Nec sumptus consumitur.

Sumunt boni, sumunt mali:
Sorte tamen inaequali,
Vitae vel interitus.

And as he hath done and planned it —
"Do this" — hear his love command it,
"For a memory of me."
Learned, Lord, in thy own science,
Bread and wine, in sweet compliance,
As a Host we offer thee.

So the Christian dogma summeth,
That the bread his flesh becometh,
And the wine his sacred blood:
Though we feel it not nor see it,
Living faith that doth decree it
All defects of sense makes good.

Lo! Beneath the species dual
(Signs, not things), is hid a jewel
Far beyond creation's reach!
Though his flesh as food abideth,
And his blood as drink — he hideth
Undivided under each.

Whoso eateth it can never
Break the body, rend or sever;
Christ entire our hearts doth fill:
Thousands eat the bread of heaven,
Yet as much to one is given:
Christ, though eaten, bideth still.

Good and bad, they come to greet him:
Unto life the former eat him,
And the latter unto death;

Mors est malis, vita bonis:
Vide paris sumptionis
Quam sit dispar exitus.

Fracto demum sacramento,
Ne vacilles, sed memento
Tantum esse sub fragmento,
Quantum tot tegitur.
Nulla rei fit scissura:
Signi tantum fit fractura,
Qua nec status, nec statura
Signati minuitur.

Ecce panis angelorum,
Factus cibus viatorum:
Vere Panis filiorum,
Non mittendus canibus.
In figuris praesignatur,
Cum Isaac immolatur,
Agnus Paschae deputatur,
Datur manna patribus.

Bone Pastor, panis vere,
Iesu, nostri miserere:
Tu nos pasce, nos tuere,
Tu nos bona fac videre
In terra viventium.
Tu qui cuncta scis et vales,
Qui nos pascis hic mortales:
Tuos ibi commensales,
Cohaeredes et sodales
Fac sanctorum civium.

These find death and those find heaven;
See, from the same life-seed given,
How the harvest differeth!

When at last the bread is broken,
Doubt not what the Lord hath spoken:
In each part the same love-token,
The same Christ, our hearts adore:
For no power the thing divideth —
'Tis the symbols he provideth,
While the Savior still abideth
Undiminished as before.

Hail, angelic bread of heaven
Now the pilgrim's hoping-leaven,
Yea, the bread to children given
That to dogs must not be thrown:
In the figures contemplated
'Twas with Isaac immolated,
By the lamb 'twas antedated,
In the manna it is known.

O Good Shepherd, still confessing
Love, in spite of our transgressing —
Here thy blessed food possessing,
Make us share thine every blessing
In the land of life and love:
Thou, whose power hath all completed
And thy flesh as food hath meted
Make us, at thy table seated,
By thy saints as friends be greeted,
In thy paradise above.

—TRANSLATION BY H.T. HENRY

I. Praise!

Praise, O Zion, praise thy Savior!

St. Thomas begins his eucharistic hymns by urging us to praise: *Praise, O Zion, praise thy Savior!* Praise, indeed, is perhaps the purest form of prayer. Unlike prayers of petition, praise seeks nothing in return. Unlike prayers of thanksgiving, praise does not depend upon benefits we've already received from God. In praise we honor God for who he is, rather than what he can do for us.

This is the way the angels pray. "Holy, holy, holy, is the Lord God Almighty!" (Rev 4:8). "Glory to God in the highest!" (Lk 2:14). It is for praise that the angels were created. Praise defines their life.

We, however, tend to seek the Lord when we need something, or we turn to him happily when we're grateful. And so we should. But how often do we approach him simply to worship him?

It's not that God needs our praise. It is, rather, we who need to praise God. In one of the prayers of the Mass, the priest says: "You made man . . . to praise you day by day for the marvels of your wisdom and power." Like the angels, we were created for the purpose of praise, and we feel unfulfilled if we neglect it.

Praise is not flattery. Flattery implies a hidden motive behind insincere words. To God, no thought lies hidden. He knows our motives, he knows our needs, before we put them into words.

St. Thomas said: "We use words in speaking to God, not to make known our thoughts to him who is the searcher of hearts, but that we may bring ourselves and our hearers to give reverence to him. . . . We need to praise God with our lips, not for his sake, but for our own sake."

Praise him, now, from whom all blessings flow.

☩

2. Zion

Praise, O Zion!

To share in the prayer of St. Thomas, we must learn to read the Bible as he did. For Thomas, sacred history showed God's fatherly care for his people, evident from the beginning of time. Thus, throughout the Old Testament God foreshadowed the work of redemption he would eventually complete in the New Testament. When Thomas read the Bible, he saw the New Testament concealed in the Old, and the Old Testament revealed in the New. Tradition calls this method of reading "typology."

A *type* is an Old Testament foreshadowing of a New Testament person, place, object, or event. St. Peter says, for example, that our baptism was prefigured by the ancient flood in the time of Noah (1 Pet 3:20-21). St. Paul saw the Passover lamb as a type of Christ (1 Cor 5:7).

The apostles learned to read the Old Testament this way from Jesus, who, "beginning with Moses and all the prophets . . . interpreted to them in *all* the Scriptures the things concerning himself. . . . '[E]verything written about me in the law of Moses and the prophets and the psalms must be fulfilled' " (Lk 24:27, 44; emphasis added).

From the first generation, Christians saw Zion as a type of the Church. Zion was the hilltop in Jerusalem from which King David reigned. Christ, in turn, as the Son of David, reigns as king in his Church. It was in a home on Mount Zion that Jesus celebrated the Last Supper, the first Eucharist, with his apostles.

The Church, then, is the new Zion, especially when it gathers for the Mass: "You have come to Mount Zion and to the city of the living God, the heavenly Jerusalem . . . and to the assembly of the first-born who are enrolled in heaven . . . and to Jesus, the mediator of a new covenant, and to the sprinkled blood that speaks more graciously than the blood of Abel" (Heb 12:22-24).

Before the Eucharist, now — praise, O Zion, praise your Savior!

✠

3. The Bread of Life

Living bread and bread life-bringing.

St. Thomas alludes to Jesus' great eucharistic sermon in John's gospel. "I am the living bread which came down from heaven. . . . The bread which I shall give for the life of the world is my flesh" (Jn 6:51). Preached in the synagogue of Capernaum, this sermon baffled its hearers. " 'How can this man give us his flesh to eat? . . . This is a hard saying. Who can listen to it?' . . . After this many of his disciples drew back and no longer went about with him" (Jn 6:52, 60, 66).

Jesus' Real Presence in the Eucharist was, for the disciples unwilling to believe him, the great stumbling block. Yet he proceeded with his eternal plan for the institution of the sacrament. "On the night when he was betrayed [he] took bread, and when he had given thanks, he broke it, and said, 'This is my body which is for you. Do this in remembrance of me' " (1 Cor 11:23-24).

In St. Thomas's day, the Real Presence remained a "hard saying" for some. Even within the Christian Church, new heresies sprang up, claiming that Jesus' presence was merely symbolic. Thomas devoted many hundreds of pages to refuting these notions and clarifying the doctrine of Jesus: that he is truly present — Body, Blood, Soul, and Divinity — under the appearances of bread and wine.

Though the Host may be broken, Christ's body cannot be divided. Whoever receives a particle of the

Host, receives the whole Christ, even though hundreds receive him at a given Mass.

On his deathbed, Thomas gazed upon the Host and made a profession of faith in the Eucharist, and we today can make it our own: "Even were it possible for us wayfarers through life to have some greater knowledge of this truth than sincere faith gives us — faith inexpressibly true — yet now in that faith alone I declare that I truly believe and most certainly know that this is indeed true God and Man, Son of the eternal Father, born of the Virgin mother, the Lord Jesus Christ. This I sincerely believe and profess."

✠

4. At Table

At the Lord's own table given
To the twelve as bread from heaven . . .

It was fitting, said St. Thomas, for Jesus to give us himself in forms of common food: bread and wine. Both were staples of any family meal in Judea during Jesus' life — and in Italy and France during Thomas's life. And Thomas presents the Last Supper as a family meal. The Latin word the poet uses is not "the twelve," as we see in the English translation, but "the brothers" — *fratrum*. The apostles were brothers; they were a family.

God has made himself known to us, and has even given his body and blood to us, in these common forms. We cannot live without air; and God has revealed himself as Spirit, a word whose Hebrew root also means breath, wind, and air. We cannot live without the cooling, cleansing, and moistening properties of water; God gives us new life through water in baptism. We cannot live without the sustenance of food, our "daily bread"; and God has given himself as bread from heaven.

Life is unimaginable, and indeed unlivable, without these basic things: breath, water, and bread. So a fully human life — a spiritual life — is impossible without the spiritual breath, water, and bread that Christ came to give the world. "Unless you eat the flesh of the Son of man and drink his blood, you have no life in you" (Jn 6:53).

Bread and wine are the right stuff for the sacrament of the Eucharist, which Christ continues to give us in the course of a ritual family meal. They are common, ordinary food and drink, the sort of everyday fare that has sustained individuals from the dawn of civilization. But, more importantly — and for just as long — these common things, bread and wine, have comprised the meals that have made families. Food sustains us, but meals do more. Meals unite us in households and families. At the common table of the Lord — at the Mass — we are all *fratrum*, children of a common Father, brothers and sisters of the Lord Jesus. "The children share in flesh and blood" (Heb 2:14).

☩

5. The New Passover

At the new King's sacred table,
The new Law's new Pasch is able
To succeed the ancient rite:
Old to new its place hath given,
Truth has far the shadows driven,
Darkness flees before the light.

In his poems and in his theology, St. Thomas gives as much attention to the Old Testament types of the Eucharist as he gives to their New Testament fulfillment. He saw the two Testaments as but a single revelation of God's providence. What God promised, he fulfilled, but only after he had prepared his people. This preparation appears most clearly in the Old Testament foreshadowings. Thus, in the "Lauda, Sion," Thomas speaks of the sacrifice of Isaac as a sign of the sacrifice of the Mass. The manna in the desert he treats as a foretaste of the sacrament. But, of all the eucharistic types, Thomas considered the most important to be the Passover, or Pasch (from the Hebrew *Pesach*).

Passover marked the high point of the Jewish liturgical year — the festival that commemorated God's deliverance of his chosen people from slavery in Egypt. On Passover night, the seventh plague fell upon the oppressive and obstinate Egyptians: God's angel struck down the firstborn son in every household. The children of Israel were spared because they had eaten a sacred meal prescribed by God — a meal of lamb and unleavened bread — and they had smeared the lamb's blood on their doorposts. The angel of the Lord "passed over" the houses so marked.

Jesus instituted the Eucharist in the course of a Passover meal. He took the traditional unleavened bread and pronounced it to be his body. He took the traditional libation of wine and pronounced it to be his blood. Moreover, Christ became our lamb of sacrifice. "Christ, our Paschal lamb, has been sacrificed," said St. Paul. "Let us, therefore, celebrate the festival . . . with the unleavened bread of sincerity and truth" (1 Cor 5:8).

As the lamb of God, Christ is the perfect offering on our behalf. He is the price of our redemption from slavery to sin; he has saved us from certain death. As the firstborn of ancient Israel were spared by the blood of the lamb, so are we, by the blood of Christ. We are the firstborn of the New Israel, the Church, which is the "assembly of the firstborn" (Heb 12:23).

Celebrate now with him, the unleavened bread of sincerity and truth.

✠

6. Dogma

So the Christian dogma summeth,
That the bread his flesh becometh,
And the wine his sacred blood:
Though we feel it not nor see it,
Living faith that doth decree it
All defects of sense makes good.

The feast of Corpus Christi celebrates a marvel: Jesus Christ, true God and true man, gives himself to the Church as spiritual food. "My flesh is food indeed" (Jn 6:55). The Church proclaims this marvel through the dogma of transubstantiation. It's a mighty word to describe a mightier reality.

What the Church teaches, Thomas explains in compact detail, in these verses and in the *Summa Theologica*. In fact, the verses of the "Lauda, Sion" closely track the explanations of the Eucharist found in questions 73-83 of the Third Part of the *Summa*.

When the priest pronounces the words of consecration, the bread becomes the flesh of Jesus Christ, the wine becomes his blood. After that moment, there is no longer a crumb we can call bread or a drop we can call wine. The very substance has changed, though the appearance has remained the same. What tastes and smells and looks like bread is Christ; what tastes and smells and looks like wine is Christ.

The species of bread and wine each contain the whole Christ: Body, Blood, Soul, and Divinity. In Communion, then, his heart becomes our heart, his sinews ours, too. Yet, though we consume the Host, Christ's body is never divided. And, though thousands consume Christ, each consumes him entire.

Thomas leaves no room for a symbolic interpretation of the sacrament. His language is graphically realistic, speaking of flesh and blood. Christ said: "This is my body," Thomas explains, and "this would not be true if the substance of the bread were to remain there; for the substance of bread never is the body of Christ." If the bread had remained bread, Jesus would instead have told the apostles, "Here is my body" — here, *with* the bread.

But instead he told them: *This is my body.*

The change comes about by Christ's words, which are spoken by the priest. The last instant of pronouncing the words is the first instant in which Christ's body is in the sacrament.

Many people today dismiss dogma as if it were cold formula. But nothing could be further from Thomas's view. Dogma is the way we begin to understand a marvel that is otherwise beyond our understanding. The dogma of transubstantiation is a living truth with a beating heart — a heart you share with Jesus Christ.

Taste and see the goodness of the Lord. Give thanks to the Lord for he is good.

✠

7. Angels' Food

Hail, angelic bread of heaven
Now the pilgrim's hoping-leaven,
Yea, the bread to children given
That to dogs must not be thrown.

The "Lauda, Sion" draws to a dramatic, even explosive conclusion with the final two verses, which bring together all the poem's dogmatic and biblical themes. Old Testament and New Testament allusions arise like fireworks, one immediately after another, in short, spectacular, illuminating bursts.

The next-to-last verse, reproduced on this page, begins with an evocation of Psalm 78 — "Man ate of the bread of the angels; he sent them food in abundance" (v. 25) — which is itself an evocation of the miraculous rain of manna from the sky in Exodus (ch. 16). Both Jesus (Jn 6:31–50) and St. Paul (1 Cor 10:3) had spoken of manna as a foreshadowing of the Eucharist. Thomas follows them, suggesting again the Exodus themes of redemption, deliverance, and fatherly care. Unlike manna, however, the Eucharist feeds more than the belly. The Eucharist fills the soul to overflowing. In heaven, the angels enjoy a feast of contemplation, gazing upon God in his very essence. In Holy Communion, we take part in the heavenly feast; indeed, we go to heaven, even here on earth. And God enables us a communion that even the angels cannot enjoy: We mingle ourselves with him; we are partakers of his very nature (2 Pt 1:4), his Body and Blood, Soul, and Divinity.

Now for us — as, long ago, for the Israelites in the desert — the angels' bread has become pilgrims' bread. Now, however, our Promised Land is not Canaan, but heaven. And if we would consider ourselves pilgrims, we must make the effort to advance toward that Promised Land. If we would take the pilgrim's food, we must be free of mortal sin; for sin is a turning away from our goal, which is God. If we are to take the pilgrim's food, we should be advancing, as pilgrims — or at least striving to advance — in holiness, wisdom, and virtue. For there is no standing still in the spiritual life. If we are not moving forward, we are falling backward. And backsliding means slipping away from the divine nature — which is ours by the grace of our baptism as children of God — and into an animal existence, unworthy of the Eucharist. "It is not fair," Jesus said, "to take the children's bread and throw it to the dogs" (Mt 15:26).

Are you doing all you can to receive Communion worthily? Do you have an effective plan, including prayer, study, and sacrifice, for advancing on the way to heaven?

✠

II.

Pange, Lingua

Sing, My Tongue, the Savior's Glory

Pange Lingua

Pange, lingua, gloriosi
Corporis mysterium,
Sanguinisque pretiosi,
Quem in mundi pretium,
Fructus ventris generosi,
Rex effudit gentium.

Nobis datus, nobis natus
Ex intacta Virgine,
Et in mundo conversatus
Sparso verbi semine,
Sui moras incolatus
Miro clausit ordine.

In supremae nocte coenae,
Recumbens cum fratribus.
Observata lege plene
Cibis in legalibus,
Cibum turbae duodenae
Se dat suis manibus.

Verbum caro, panem verum
Verbo carnem efficit,
Fitque sanguis Christi merum;
Et si sensus deficit,
Ad firmandum cor sincerum
Sola fides sufficit.

Sing, My Tongue, the Savior's Glory

Sing, my tongue, the Savior's glory,
Of his flesh the mystery sing;
Of the blood, all price excelling,
Shed by our immortal King.
Destined for the world's redemption
From a noble womb to spring.

Of a pure and spotless Virgin
Born for us on earth below,
He, as man with man conversing,
Stayed the seeds of truth to sow;
Then he closed in solemn order
Wondrously his life of woe.

On the night of that Last Supper
Seated with his chosen band,
He the paschal victim eating,
First fulfils the Law's command;
Then as food to all his brethren
Gives himself with his own hand.

Word made flesh! The bread of nature
By his word to flesh he turns;
Wine into his blood he changes:
What though sense no change discerns,
Only be the heart in earnest,
Faith her lesson quickly learns.

Tantum ergo Sacramentum
Veneremur cernui:
Et antiquum documentum
Novo cedat ritui:
Praestet fides supplementum
Sensuum defectui.

Genitori, Genitoque
Laus et iubilatio,
Salus, honor, virtus quoque
Sit et benedictio:
Procedenti ab utroque
Compar sit laudatio. Amen.

Down in adoration falling,
Lo! The sacred Host we hail;
Lo! O'er ancient forms departing,
Newer rites of grace prevail;
Faith for all defects supplying,
Where the feeble senses fail.

To the everlasting Father,
And the Son who reigns on high,
With the Holy Ghost proceeding
Forth from each eternally,
Be salvation, honor blessing,
Might and endless majesty! Amen.

— TRANSLATION BY EDWARD CASWALL

8. Sing!

Sing, my tongue, the Savior's glory,
Of his flesh the mystery sing.

Melodies move the soul, St. Thomas said, so they are particularly useful as prayers of praise. Music can inspire devotion in people who are otherwise weak in faith. Thomas cited the example of St. Augustine, who said of a stage in his conversion: "I wept in your hymns and canticles, touched to the quick by the voices of your sweet-singing Church."

Augustine held that "to sing is to pray twice," and Thomas surely agreed, for he himself recommended singing as a remedy for distraction in prayer: "If the singer sings for the sake of devotion, he pays more attention to what he says." Melody makes us linger over the words and dwell upon them, savoring them. This is one reason why St. Thomas's poems speak to millions of us who could never comprehend his theology. They have been set, by great composers, to some of history's most memorable melodies. In the "Lauda, Sion," Thomas urges his congregation to praise God "in hymn and canticle." Here again, in the "Pange, Lingua," he exhorts himself (and us) to "Sing!"

Today, we live amid a surfeit of music. When we drive, when we shop, when we ride the elevator or sit in a dentist's chair, our minds are occupied with piped-in popular songs. And the melodies, together with their lyrics, tend to remain with us long after the song has ended. Even obnoxious music has a way of doing that, and even bad melodies move the soul — but where?

We need to ask ourselves what sort of songs occupy our minds, and where do their lyrics focus our attention. Consider whether your soul would be better moved if you spent more time singing, or listening to, songs that glorify God.

9. Glory

Sing, my tongue, the Savior's glory,
Of his flesh the mystery sing;
Of the blood, all price excelling,
Shed by our immortal King.

In this song, we sing the glory of the Savior's blood. For his blood has redeemed us from the everlasting death we have earned by our sins. Christ is our Savior, and the Eucharist is the ordinary way we receive the effects of his salvation. "This is the bread which comes down from heaven, that a man may eat of it and not die" (Jn 6:50).

Yet Christ has saved us not just *from* the spiritual death of sin. He has saved us *for glory*. He has not only restored our human dignity and integrity; he has enabled us to live with the freedom of God's own children. He has given us his life, that we may share with the Son in the life of the Trinity.

"If anyone eats of this bread, he will live forever; and the bread which I shall give for the life of the world is my flesh" (Jn 6:51). The life he gives us — eternal life — is the life of glory.

Christ gave us this glory by means of his redeeming death. "He is the mediator of a new covenant, so that those who are called may receive the promised eternal inheritance, since a death has occurred which redeems them . . ." (Heb 9:25).

Christ's suffering was enough to win us glory, yet not so that we are automatically admitted to glory. We must first "suffer with him in order that we may also be glorified with him" (Rom 8:17).

The Eucharist gives us the power to travel onward to glory. That's why it's called "Viaticum," or "pilgrim's food." But we cannot come to glory through the sacrament if we receive it unworthily. Thomas quotes St. Augustine: "The sacrament is one thing, the power of the sacrament another." Many people receive the sacrament with mortal sins on their souls, and by the very act of receiving they bring death upon themselves. "Whoever, therefore, eats the bread or drinks the cup of the Lord in an unworthy manner," said St. Paul, "will be guilty of profaning the body and blood of the Lord. . . . That is why . . . some of you have died" (1 Cor 11:27, 30).

Augustine and Thomas urge us to "bring innocence to the altar." For those who do not keep innocence, do not secure the effect of this sacrament.

We restore our innocence through the sacrament of reconciliation and penance. But our restoration begins with the grace of repentance. Let us ask God, now, for that grace. In his presence, let us examine our conscience and prepare to confess our sins. Again, Christ comes to save us — from our sins, and for glory.

☩

10. The Ancient Law

On the night of that Last Supper
Seated with his chosen band,
He the paschal victim eating,
First fulfills the Law's command.

Some Christians mistakenly believe that Jesus came to reject or abolish the religion of Israel. Yet we see, in this verse of St. Thomas, that Jesus carefully obeyed the Law. Christ revered the ancient Law of Israel, even as he fulfilled it and perfected it. "Think not that I have come to abolish the Law and the prophets; I have come not to abolish them but to fulfill them. For truly, I say to you, till heaven and earth pass away, not an iota, not a dot, will pass away from the Law until all is accomplished" (Mt 5:17–18).

Jesus and his apostles followed the Law because the Law's primary purpose was to prepare the way for Christ. St. Paul said that the Law was our "custodian" until Christ came. Israel's Law was like a shadow cast backward from Jesus. We can discern something about an object from the shadow it casts; but much remains in obscurity.

For many centuries, the people of Israel strictly kept the Law and the Passover. The demanding precepts of the Law bespeak the importance of the life and the ritual they prescribe. The Law reigned with tremendous dignity — a dignity revered by Jesus, St. Paul, and St. Thomas.

St. Thomas wrote of the Passover laws as a "sacrament" of Christ's Passion. "It was necessary that there should be at all times among men something to show forth Our Lord's Passion; the chief sacrament of which in the old Law was the Paschal lamb.

"But," he goes on, "its successor under the New Testament is the sacrament of the Eucharist, which is a remembrance of the Passion now past, just as the other was figurative of the Passion to come. And so it was fitting that when the hour of the Passion arrived, Christ should institute a new sacrament after celebrating the old."

The sacrifices of the old Law were a mighty and imposing shadow of the true sacrifice of Christ's Passion. "For . . . the law has but a shadow of the good things to come instead of the true form of these realities" (Heb 10:1). Thus the sacrifice of the new Law — the Gospel — gives us something more, namely, Christ himself crucified, not only in signs or figures, types or shadows, but also in truth.

As we pray before the Eucharist — the fulfillment of the ancient sacrament — let us give thanks for the faithful people of Israel, for the Law, and for the Passover. Let us pray, too, for a deep love of the religion of Israel; for, in the words of Pope Pius XI, "Spiritually, we are Semites."

☩

✠

11. Word Made Flesh

Word made flesh! The bread of nature
By his word to flesh he turns.

The great Anglican hymn-writer John Mason Neale referred to this verse as the translator's cross. In the original Latin, it is a masterpiece of poetic art — rich in word-play, yet dense with meaning. So sure is Thomas, in both his theology and his verse-making, that he can speak volumes in just a handful of words. He can be playful with language, but without wasting a word. The eighteenth-century French poet Jean de Santeul said that he would trade all the work of his lifetime for this single stanza of St. Thomas.

Implicit in these six lines is the entire prologue to St. John's gospel: "In the beginning was the Word, and the Word was with God, and the Word was God. . . . All things were made through him. . . . And the Word became flesh and dwelt among us" (Jn 1:1, 3, 14).

Through the Word of God, all things were made. God spoke — "Let there be light" (Gen 1:3) — and when he spoke, his word made worlds and stars, oceans and atoms out of nothing.

When the Word was made flesh, he spoke and his word — "This is my body" — worked a wonder greater than the creation of the universe. His word changed bread to his body, wine to his blood.

St. Ambrose marveled at this power: "As soon as the consecration takes place, the bread becomes the body of Christ. How can this be done? By the consecration. The consecration takes place by means of what words? By those of the Lord Jesus. Indeed, what was said up to now was said by the priest. But here he uses the words of Christ. What is the word of Christ? It is that by which all things were made."

God did not need to become a man in order to save us. He could have redeemed us by simply speaking a word. But he knew it was best and most fitting that he become a man.

In the same way, at the time of his ascension, he could have merely assured us of his spiritual presence, and perhaps that would have been sufficient. "I am with you always, to the close of the age" (Mt 28:20). But he thought it best to remain with us incarnate.

The Word was made flesh; and the bread, by his word, is made the flesh of the Word. The Eucharist is the extension of Christ's incarnation through every time and place. In his body, he comes to embrace not only a handful of people in a particular time and place, but you and me as well.

The mystery is so great that it defies all human faculties but praise and thanksgiving, which Thomas exudes in the "Pange, Lingua." Let us take his words as our own.

✠

✝

12. Adoration

Down in adoration falling,
Lo! The sacred Host we hail

Adoration refers to the special honor we give to God alone. People who adore someone or something other than God commit the grave sin of idolatry.

Adoration is an important word, because it represents a duty we owe to God. Yet it is a word that has lost its edge in English. Popular music uses "adoration" to describe the intense feelings of a teenager for his date: "My eyes adored you. . . . Though, a million miles away from me, you couldn't see that I adored you."

Surely, the singer did not intend to commit idolatry with his song. But adoration is a word that deserves protection and preservation. We might begin our prayer today with a resolution never to misuse this word; for it has no replacement. And, again, it is an important word.

We owe God our adoration. We can even say that he longs for this attention. Jesus said to the Samaritan woman: "If you knew the gift of God" that has come your way (Jn 4:10). *If only you knew!*

More people today need to learn the meaning of the word adoration; but, more importantly, people need to learn the best ways to offer adoration. If you are praying in the presence of Our Lord in the Blessed Sacrament, then you have discovered the secret. You know the gift of God that has come your way. Now you must share the gift with others.

In the sacrament of the altar, after the words of consecration, there is nothing else but the body and the blood of Christ. Thus, St. Thomas quotes St. Ambrose, who said that "after the blessing the body [must] be adored with adoration of *latria*." *Latria* is the theological term for the worship that may be given only to God — and to no one and nothing else — not even the most exalted of creatures.

Our worship of the sacred Host expresses our trust in the promises of Jesus Christ, who said that he would give his flesh as the bread of life. With our worship of the sacred Host, we say, too, that we believe in the power of the Creator, who pronounced the words: "This is my body."

Our faith in the Real Presence is a profound belief in God's power, in Jesus' divinity, and in the truth of the Gospel. For if the Eucharist contained real bread, we could not offer it adoration.

How good it is when parishes and religious houses offer perpetual adoration of the Blessed Sacrament. How good it is to arrive for adoration with many friends and neighbors who give God the worship he wishes, the worship he is due.

✠

13. The Mass

Newer rites of grace prevail.

Thomas's devotion to the Eucharist was profound. His brother Dominicans recalled that he would spend long hours on his knees before the tabernacle. When he faced a particularly difficult problem, he would go up to the tabernacle and lean his large forehead against it, as if to rest against the Master's heart, as did the beloved disciple at the Last Supper (Jn 13:23).

But Thomas invested his greatest fervor not in private adoration, nor in his theological study, but in his devotion to the Mass — the Lord's new rite of grace. For it was the Mass that the Lord established as his memorial: "Do this in remembrance of me" (Lk 22:19). And the Host — either exposed in the monstrance or reserved in the tabernacle — was, first of all, the fruit of the Mass.

Throughout his adult life, Thomas said Mass every day, unless prevented by illness. In addition, he would attend — and usually serve — a Mass said by another friar.

According to his first biographer, Bernard Gui, Thomas said Mass devoutly, "utterly absorbed in the mystery." At the moment when he or the other priest would elevate the Host, he would pray, in Latin: *Tu Rex Gloriae, Christe, Tu Patris sempiternus es Filius.* "O Christ, You are the King of Glory, You are the eternal Son of the Father."

The culmination of his experience, though, was Holy Communion, at which Thomas's "face ran with tears."

Thomas's parents had consecrated him to the religious life when he was six years old. From that time, he lived in a Benedictine abbey and daily prayed the liturgy with the monks. He died just short of his fiftieth birthday. It is likely, then, that he attended well over thirty-two thousand Masses in his life. From an early age, he had grown intimately familiar with the small details of the ritual. Yet the Mass never seemed to grow old for him. It always remained a new rite of grace, an experience so startling as to move the friar to tears.

May we grow in our understanding of the Mass. May we be frequent and devout in our attendance. But may we never grow tired of the rite.

Jesus, give us the grace you gave Thomas: to make the Mass ever new to our hearts.

✠

☩

14. Feeble Senses

Faith for all defects supplying,
Where the feeble senses fail.

Are the senses really feeble? There are some religions and philosophies that distrust the senses. Their teachers claim that the senses convey nothing but illusion. Some even teach that the senses are completely corrupt and evil, as is the world they behold.

Such teachers lived in Thomas's day, and some called themselves Christians. But Thomas would have none of it. He held the senses to be the first organs of knowledge. "Our reason," he said, "has its origin in the senses." And elsewhere: "the principle of knowledge is in the senses." Because God created us with a soul united to a body, it is impossible for us to understand anything unless we base our understanding on the data collected by our eyes, ears, nose, tongue, and fingertips.

God created the world and saw that it was good. We live in this world, and we, too, must see its goodness. But to do so, we must first trust our seeing.

So why did Thomas call the senses "feeble"?

The answer is that we must not expect to get the whole truth from our senses. Along with our external senses, we also need the light of the intellect. It is our intellect that reflects on the data of our senses and uses it to make abstract and universal conclusions. I see and hear and smell a dog; then I can think about what a dog is.

God made us to gather knowledge in a certain, particular way. This is how we get to know the world God made, and it is through our knowledge of the world that we begin to know the world's Creator. From the artwork, we begin to glimpse the mind of the artist. Moreover, God made us with senses and reason to engage the world, and he made the world in order to delight our senses and reason. Thomas placed such a high value on the senses that he declared it a vice for a man to be completely unsensual, incapable of enjoying the world.

But we must also understand that there's more to life than meets the eye. And there are truths that surpasses the limits of our intellect. That truth is the object of faith. Faith is not contrary to the senses but concerns things that sense does not reach.

In the sacrament, Christ's body is substantially present. But "substance" — which, by definition, is what a thing *is* — is not something visible to the eye. Before this divine reality, we are like nocturnal animals whose eyes are suddenly blinded by the light of day.

Faith, however, makes up for our lack. "The apostles said to Jesus: 'Increase our faith!' " (Lk 17:5). Let this be our prayer as we gaze upon the Lord with the eyes he gave us.

☦

III.

Sacris Solemniis

With Joy This Festal Day

Sacris Solemniis

Sacris solemniis juncta sint gaudia,
Et ex praecordiis sonent praeconia
Recedant vetera, nova sint omnia,
Corda, voces, et opera.

Noctis recolitur coena novissima,
Qua Christus creditur agnum et azyma
Dedisse fratribus, juxta legitima
Priscis indulta patribus.

Post agnum typicum, expletis epulis,
Corpus Dominicum datum discipulis,
Sic totum omnibus, quod totum singulis,
Ejus fatemur manibus.

Dedit fragilibus corporis ferculum,
Dedit et tristibus sanguinis poculum,
Dicens: Accipite quod trado vasculum,
Omnes ex eo bibite.

Sic sacrificium istud instituit,
Cujus officium committi voluit
Solis presbyteris, quibus sic congruit,
Ut sumant, et dent ceteris.

With Joy This Festal Day

With joy this festal day let all the heavens ring,
And what the lip shall say be the heart's heralding,
And, as the old departs, renewed be everything,
Voices and labors, hymns and hearts!

For now do we recall the supper of that night
When to his brethren all the Lord of gracious
  might
The lamb and azyme-bread gave in the olden rite
By Israel's fathers chronicled.

Then lo, the typic board bears what it but foretold;
His body did the Lord give to the twelve: behold,
Himself entire to each, while all entirely hold,
Christ gave, as holy faith doth teach.

He gave to weakness then the strength of
  heavenly food;
To the sad hearts of men, wine of a gracious flood;
Saying: Receive ye this, the chalice of my blood;
O drink ye all — my blood it is.

The Savior in this wise did for our lowly sake
Ordain the sacrifice, and of its office make
The new Law's priest possessed, who should the
  first partake,
And then distribute to the rest.

Panis angelicus fit panis hominum;
Dat panis caelicus figuris terminum:
O res mirabilis, manducat Dominum
Pauper, servus, et humilis.

Te, trina Deitas unaque, poscimus,
Sic nos tu visita, sicut te colimus,
Per tuas semitas duc nos quo tendimus,
Ad lucem, quam inhabitas.

The very angels' bread doth food to men afford;
The types have vanished, remains the truth adored:
O wondrous mystery! Their banquet is the
    Lord —
The poor and lowly, bond and free.

O God forever blest, O Three in One, we pray:
Visit the longing breast, enter this house of clay,
And lead us through the night unto the perfect
    day,
Where dwellest thou in endless light!

— Translation by H.T. Henry

✠

15. This Glad Solemnity

With joy this festal day let all the heavens ring,
And what the lip shall say be the heart's heralding.

This poem, "Sacris Solemniis," makes demands that
seem contradictory to modern ears. Here Thomas bids
us, according to one translation, to "Welcome with
jubilee this glad solemnity." Another interpretation
renders it: "At this our solemn feast, let holy joys
abound."

We are unaccustomed, however, to consider *joy*
and *solemnity* in the same breath. Today's culture — in
advertising, television, and popular music — tends to
identify joy with the free indulgence of guilty pleasures. Solemnity we equate with somberness and bore-
dom. On weekends and vacations, we tend to eat too
much; perhaps we drink too much. If we must go to
church, then prayer and sermons, like work, are something to be endured.

But the modern round of work and weekend is
uniformly joyless. We offer our work as a sacrifice for
the sake of a weekend; and our weekends, though
filled with momentary pleasures, leave us sick from
bodily excess, with no lasting happiness.

The old-time Christian, in the middle of a fast,
knew greater joy than the modern American, because
his fasts had a sublime purpose. He gave up a sensate
pleasure so that his soul could turn, instead, to God.
He fasted for the same reason he worked; he fasted

for the same reason he feasted. He worked and fasted and feasted, all in due season, for the sake of love.

For Christians like St. Thomas, all life burns with the fire of that single passion: The consuming love of God. Such love is a serious matter; its rituals are solemn occasions. But, even at its most solemn, love is never joyless. In fact, love is the only thing that gives us lasting joy. What men and women today call joys are, by contrast, the fleeting, sensate pleasures of feeding animals.

When Christians, however, enjoy the same sensory experience — the taste of good wine or thick steak, the aroma of a pipe, the warmth of a spouse's embrace — we do so for the sake of God's glory. On a feast day, we feast in order to celebrate something divine. We bless our bodily senses with our feasting — all with proper solemnity.

C.S. Lewis wrote that our Christian feasts are, indeed, supposed to be more solemn than our fasts. Easter is called "solemn"; Good Friday is not. Corpus Christi is a solemnity. The solemn, Lewis explained, is "the festal which is also the stately and the ceremonial, the proper occasion for pomp." At a solemn feast, we "wear unusual clothes and move with calculated dignity." We forget ourselves, we lose ourselves, in the beauty of the ritual.

Learn, then, to "celebrate the festival!" (1 Cor 5:8). Lose yourself for a moment, that you may gain heaven forever.

☩

16. Unleavened Bread

The lamb and azyme-bread . . .
By Israel's fathers chronicled.

The Feast of Corpus Christi had its origin when Christ appeared to Blessed Juliana of Mont Cornillon. He told her of his wish for a feast day in honor of the Eucharist, adding that this special feast had always been in the mind of the blessed Trinity.

The idea was with God from all eternity. It was there when he made his covenants with Israel's patriarchs; and so it appeared, though in a shadowy way, throughout the Old Testament. These foreshadows are the "types" or "figures" St. Thomas loved to evoke.

One such figure is the unleavened bread hastily baked by the Israelites on the eve of their exodus from Egypt (Ex 12:15, 19). (The Latin word for unleavened is *azymus*, and this sometimes appears in English as *azyme*.) Jews in every succeeding generation have observed seven days without leaven in commemoration of the Exodus.

The ancients discerned in leaven a symbol of moral corruption. For a while, yeast had even been counted among the unclean foods, because its rot could destroy an entire harvest. Jesus himself used the word *leaven* in a pejorative way: "Beware of the leaven of the Pharisees" (Mt 16:6). Left unrepented, sin, like leaven, spreads its rot rapidly through the soul.

Unleavened bread, on the other hand, stood for purity and integrity — dough that is untainted, unmixed.

Jesus' Last Supper took place "on the first day of Unleavened Bread" (Mt. 26:17). So the bread that Jesus consecrated was azyme bread. This is why the Western church, as well as the Maronite and Armenian churches, continues to use unleavened bread in its Eucharist — to represent the historic event most accurately.

Thomas acknowledged, in his *Summa*, the dignity of the Eastern tradition of using leavened bread in the Eucharist. But he found his own Church's custom satisfying — first, because Christ used unleavened bread; second, because "uncorrupted" bread suggested the sinlessness of Christ; and third, because of the testimony of St. Paul: "Christ, our Paschal lamb, has been sacrificed. Let us, therefore, celebrate the festival, not with the old leaven, the leaven of malice and evil, but with the unleavened bread of sincerity and truth" (1 Cor 5:7-8).

May our Communion with Christ make us as pure as Christ — unleavened in our sincerity, true in our virtue.

✠

17. Weak and Sad

He gave to weakness then the strength of heavenly food;
To the sad hearts of men, wine of a gracious flood.

Jesus celebrated the first Eucharist with a congregation best characterized by weakness and sadness. Within hours, these very apostles would flee in fear rather than die with their Master (Mt 26:56). Jesus could see it in their faces: "Because I have said these things to you, sorrow has filled your hearts" (Jn 16:6).

The apostles were sad, though not only because their friend had foretold his imminent death. Sadness enveloped them because they sensed they could not face the coming ordeal with courage. Their sadness was the bitter fruit of their moral weakness.

For they knew better than to give in to cowardice. They had seen Jesus work miracles. They had stood inches away as he raised the dead. They had seen him transfigured in the heavens as he spoke with Moses and Elijah.

And they knew who Jesus was. They had heard the voice from heaven say, "This is my beloved Son." Peter had boldly confessed Jesus to be the Messiah, the Son of the living God.

Yet Peter would be the apostle most conspicuously overtaken by cowardice. He would deny the Master three times.

They were sad because they found themselves too weak to behave as the men they knew themselves to be. After everything Jesus had told them, after everything he had shown them, they still found themselves dominated by an animal instinct for self-preservation, no matter the cost to the soul.

Yet the Christian life is neither an animal life nor a merely natural human life. It is a supernatural and divine life. "You are gods!" Jesus said. In baptism, we come to share in the nature of God. Thus God empowers us and *expects* us to do great things. He calls each and every Christian to the fullness of holiness. "Be perfect," Jesus said to the crowd, the rabble, "as your heavenly Father is perfect" (Mt 5:48).

Today, when Jesus celebrates the Eucharist, he looks out upon congregations of women and men who are no more courageous and no stronger than the apostles were. He looks out upon you and me, upon our friends and neighbors and co-workers. He knows that we do not always, or even often, live up to the divine life we have received in baptism.

Still, he gives us what he gave the twelve. To those weak men, he gave the bread of the strong. Their sad hearts he gladdened with heavenly wine.

He gives us all we need. For the perfection of holiness is entirely a gift from God. It's a gift freely given, but it's a gift we may freely accept or reject.

We must pray as Jesus instructed the apostles that night. "Watch and pray that you may not enter into temptation. The spirit indeed is willing, but the flesh is weak" (Mt 26:41).

☩

☩

18. Sacrifice

The Savior in this wise did for our lowly sake
Ordain the sacrifice. . . .

In the *Summa Theologica,* St. Thomas examines the various titles for the Mass: the Eucharist, the Communion, and so on. He even introduces a title still unusual in the West; he quotes St. John of Damascus, who calls the Mass "the Assumption," because, through the Mass, "we assume the Godhead of the Son." But the term he dwells longest upon is the one he uses in this poem — the term favored also by the early Christians. He calls the Mass "the Sacrifice."

What is the sacrifice we offer in the Mass? It is Jesus Christ. The Mass is a re-presentation of his suffering and death on the cross, which was itself a redeeming sacrifice. His blood paid the price of all our sins, a price that could not be paid by all the sacrifices of sinful men throughout history. Christ is the perfect victim; Christ is the perfect priest.

This does not mean that Jesus suffers and dies every time we celebrate the Eucharist. Rather, the Mass is our participation in his unique offering that took place "once for all" (Heb 9:12). In a sense, the "once" of Jesus' sacrifice was very particular: It happened around A.D. 30 (long, long ago) in the land of Palestine (far, far away). Yet in another sense, God willed that the sacrifice should be universal, and as near as every human heart, so he extended it through space and time by his institution of the Mass. Jesus is not sacrificed again and again; but we are invited again and again to participate in his once-for-all sacrifice. On the contrary, Augustine says (see *Letter* xcviii): "Christ was sacrificed once in himself, and yet he is sacrificed daily in the Sacrament."

The Book of Revelation refers to Jesus as "the lamb that was slain" from the beginning of the world (13:8). Thus, says St. Thomas, it's true to say that Christ was sacrificed even in the figures of the Old Testament, principally in the Passover lamb. Still, it was necessary that the sacrifice of the New Testament should have something more — namely, that it should contain Christ crucified, not just symbolically, but truly.

When we go to Mass, we are uniting our lives with the one sacrifice that has been offered from the beginning. When we celebrate the Mass, we are taking up Jesus' cross as our own. We are offering not only Christ, but ourselves and all that we have.

As Augustine said (in his *City of God*): Whoever offers sacrifice must share in the sacrifice, because the outward sacrifice he offers is a sign of the inner sacrifice by which he offers himself completely to God.

✠

19. Priesthood

The Savior in this wise did for our lowly sake
Ordain the sacrifice, and of its office make
The new Law's priest possessed, who should
the first partake,
And then distribute to the rest.

Reading the Gospel, St. Thomas looked upon the apostles at the Last Supper and found them to be weak, sinful, and sad. Yet, undeserving as they were, Christ gave them his body and blood. Moreover — as if that were not enough — he commissioned them to offer his sacrifice perpetually.

"Do this," he said, "in remembrance of me." And so he conferred upon his first priests the power to accomplish the Eucharist.

So great is this sacrament that it is performed only in the *person* of Christ. The priest consecrates this sacrament not by his own power, but as the minister of Jesus Christ. The Eucharist works not through the priest's merits, but through the power of Jesus, whose words the priest utters: "This is my body. . . . This is the cup of my blood."

All baptized Christians share in what is called the "common priesthood" of Christ. We receive this consecration in baptism. A devout lay person is united with Christ by spiritual union through faith and charity, though not by sacramental power. Ours is a spiritual priesthood for offering spiritual sacrifices (1 Pet 2:5). So St. Paul urged us: "Present your bodies as a living sacrifice" (Rom 12:1).

Men who receive holy orders, however, are conformed to Christ in a special way. They are identified with him most profoundly, and only they may celebrate a valid Eucharist. Theology tells us that, upon ordination, a man is changed in his very being. The priest bears Christ's image, and he pronounces the words of consecration in Christ's person and by Christ's power. Even if the priest is a grave sinner, the sacrament remains valid, because ultimately it is not the sinner who makes the offering.

It can be easy to get lost in the theory of these matters, and to forget the deeply personal dimension of the first Mass, the Last Supper. In the "Sacris Solemniis," Thomas places the doctrine of priesthood squarely in the context of Jesus' friendship with his apostles.

When death comes to part close friends, the survivor cannot help but memorize the last words of the one who died. So, says Thomas, Our Lord instituted the Eucharist at his last parting with his disciples, in order that it might be their most prized memorial of his life. "Do this," he said, "in memory of me."

Remembrance is the foundation of their priesthood. How could they ever forget? How can we?

✛

✠

20. The Poor, the Slave, the Lowly

O wondrous mystery! Their banquet is the Lord —
The poor and lowly, bond and free.

"Blessed are the poor" (Lk 6:20). These four words, the beginning of the Beatitudes, surely rank among Jesus' most shocking proclamations. By any material measure, the poor appear to be cursed. They must go through life hungry, cold, ill-clothed. In Jesus' day, as in our own, there lived many seemingly devout people, and even theologians, who believed that poverty was God's punishment for an individual's sins.

Jesus' turned this notion on its head, so that poverty became exalted and wealth disdained. "Though he was rich, yet for your sake he became poor, so that by his poverty you might become rich" (2 Cor 8:9). When the Word became flesh, he took for himself the flesh of a poor man.

Now, indeed, "The poor have good news preached to them" (Mt 11:5). God is one of them. For he gives them all he has. In his earthly ministry, Jesus associated himself with the poor, the lowly, the slaves. He *identified* himself with them. On the way to the cross, he had everything taken from him. Crucified in nakedness, he had nothing left to give but himself, and that is what he gave.

At the end of his life, he showed the very depths of meaning in the counsel he once gave to a rich young man: "Sell what you possess and give to the poor" (Mt 19:21).

In becoming a man, the Word humbled himself in poverty, left himself vulnerable to abuse, blasphemy, torture, and death. In becoming our bread, how much more has he humbled himself — vulnerable to sacrilege, rejection, and neglect.

"The poor you always have with you" (Jn 12:8), and as long as there are poor people on the earth, there will be Jesus, making his tabernacle among them.

The poor know now that God is one of them. But, more than that, God is one with them. In Holy Communion, he gives them his very life. So, while every other avenue might be closed to them, the road to heaven will be open. Indeed, the road runs wide for the poor, but impossibly narrow for the rich.

If we want to live with Jesus, we have no choice but to become poor. We need not divest ourselves of all possessions (unless that is our particular calling), but we do need to detach ourselves from them. What would happen if tomorrow we lost our savings or our home? Would we see it as the end of our lives? If so, then we would be far better off as a holy beggar who had never known these comforts.

Lacking material comfort, the poor can find comfort in God alone. Are we poor enough to afford a place at the table where the banquet is the Lord?

✝

21. Lead Us

And lead us through the night unto the perfect day.

Our Lord has much to teach us, by his humble example in the Eucharist and by his inspirations when we receive him in Holy Communion. But if we want to be taught, we must first be docile.

Docility, like "solemnity," is a word that has been degraded by recent usage. To modern ears, docility suggests mindless compliance — the easy collaboration of weak men with a despot's evil deeds. But that's not what Christians traditionally have meant by docility. Docility is, simply, a willingness to be taught.

Docility begins with humility. If we keep an accurate assessment of ourselves, we can be sure that we don't know everything. As we go about our everyday business, there's much we need to learn about law, government, medicine, media, finance — but no one has the time or the means to build such knowledge from the ground up. So we turn to others to teach us — friends, advisers, and especially older folks who have experience.

When it's a matter of our money or health, we listen attentively. Before doctors and bankers, we are docile.

Are we as docile, though, when we pray in the presence of Our Lord? Do we give him our attention in the moments after Holy Communion? Do we press him with questions as eagerly as we would press our doctors and lawyers? Do we make time for silence in his presence — silence for listening — or do we approach him mostly to tell him what we want from him?

If we want to move forward in the spiritual life, we must cultivate docility before the Lord, and also before his priests. By their office, they merit our attention, especially when we encounter them in the pulpit or the confessional.

Docility should mark our attitude toward our local bishop and the pope as well. St. Thomas was more brilliant than all the hierarchs of his day; yet he was perfectly submissive to their authority. Just before he died, he said, in the presence of the Blessed Sacrament, "I have written much on the holy body of Christ, and now I leave it all to the judgment of the holy Roman Church."

St. Thomas counsels us to apply our minds "carefully, frequently, and reverently" to the teachings of the Church and the advice of our wiser elders — "neither neglecting them through laziness, nor despising them through pride."

Only those who are docile can Christ lead "through the night unto the perfect day." As the Bible tells us, "Do not rely on your own insight" (Prov 3:5).

✠

IV.

Verbum Supernum

The Word Descending

Verbum Supernum

Verbum supernum prodiens,
Nec Patris linquens dexteram,
Ad opus suum exiens,
Venit ad vitae vesperam.

In mortem a discipulo
Suis tradendus aemulis,
Prius in vitae ferculo
Se tradidit discipulis.

Quibus sub bina specie
Carnem dedit et sanguinem;
Ut duplicis substantiae
Totum cibaret hominem.

Se nascens dedit socium,
Convescens in edulium,
Se moriens in pretium,
Se regnans dat in praemium.

O salutaris Hostia,
Quae caeli pandis ostium,
Bella premunt hostilia;
Da robur, fer auxilium.

Uni trinoque Domino
Sit sempiterna gloria:
Qui vitam sine termino
Nobis donet in patria. Amen.

The Word Descending

The Word descending from above,
Yet leaving not the Father's side,
And going to his work of love
At length had reached life's eventide.

By false disciple led to death,
That night, to envious men betrayed;
But first the Lord delivereth
Himself as his disciples' bread.

To them he gave, in twofold kind,
His very flesh, his very blood:
Of twofold substance man is made,
And he, to man, would be the food.

By birth our fellow man was he,
Our food while seated at the board;
He died, our ransomer to be;
He ever reigns, our great reward.

O saving Victim, opening wide
The gate of heaven to man below:
Our foes press on from every side;
Thine aid supply, thy strength bestow.

To thy great Name be endless praise,
Immortal Godhead, One in Three!
O grant us endless length of days
In our true native land with thee. Amen.

—TRANSLATION COMPILED FROM H.T. HENRY,
J.M. NEALE, EDWARD CASWALL, AND OTHERS

✢

22. Trinity, Incarnation, Eucharist

To thy great Name be endless praise,
Immortal Godhead, One in Three!

Those who would belittle St. Thomas usually dismiss
him as a man who reduces divine mysteries to merely
clever proofs. But nothing could be further from the
truth. Thomas did push reason to its limits — but
never beyond.

He is justifiably famous for his five ways of dem-
onstrating God's existence. Like many other philosophers, he held that nature showed ample evidence of
a Creator's design. But Thomas never claimed more
than this. He insisted, for example, that the mystery
of the Trinity could "in no way" be demonstrated.
The proofs set forth by other theologians he judged
unconvincing and improbable. "That God is three-
fold and one is solely an item of belief."

He treats the mysteries of the Incarnation and
the Eucharist in much the same way. He demonstrates
that they are not contrary to reason, but ultimately
he accepts them on the testimony of the Scriptures
and the Church. Without divine revelation, the "feeble
senses" of humanity could never arrive at these truths.
We would be more likely to see subatomic particles
without a microscope. We accept the truths of Trinity,
Incarnation, and Eucharist because they come from
an authority we trust. They come from the Scriptures

infallibly interpreted by the Church of Christ. They come, then, from Jesus Christ.

In this poem, the themes of Trinity, Incarnation, and Eucharist are interwoven, as in reality the mysteries are interwoven. The Incarnation was the definitive revelation of the Trinity. When we came to know Christ as the eternal Son, we learned also of his eternal Father; when Christ returned to the Father, he sent us the Holy Spirit.

God made us and saved us so that we should share in his Trinitarian life. The Eucharist perfects this divine life in us. United with the Son in Communion, we are necessarily united to the Father in the Spirit. Jesus prayed that all Christians may be one, "even as thou, Father, art in me, and I in thee, that they also may be in us. . . . The glory which thou hast given me, I have given to them" (Jn 17:21, 22).

These words come, of course, from Jesus' discourse at the Last Supper, the first Mass.

In the Eucharist, we receive the seeds of the glory of the Trinity; in the Eucharist, we are perfected in unity. Christ prayed for this close Communion. May we ever do the same.

✠

✠

23. Twice Blessed

To them he gave, in twofold kind,
His very flesh, his very blood:
Of twofold substance man is made,
And he, to man, would be the food.

We are neither angels nor animals. The Church teaches us that man is a creature composed of body and soul, made to the image and likeness of God. Angels do not have bodies. Animals have no immortal, spiritual soul.

When God assumed a second nature, it was not the nature of an angel or a beast. Instead, he uniquely dignified human nature, with its dual composition of soul and body. St. Thomas suggests in this stanza that Christ intended the twofold species of the Blessed Sacrament — the bread and the wine — to nourish the twofold nature of man — the body and the soul.

Thomas expands on this idea in the *Summa*, where he says that this sacrament serves to defend both the soul and the body. So Christ's body is offered under the appearance of bread for the health of the body, and his blood under the appearance of wine for the health of the soul.

God gave us the sacrament beneath a twofold veil to affect us in a powerful, symbolic way. And the division is only symbolic; for, in either species alone, the bread or the wine, we receive the whole Christ: Body, Blood, Soul, and Divinity.

The Eucharist extends God's healing power to both parts of our twofold nature. The sacrament ordinarily heals the sicknesses of our spirit. Every Holy Communion blots out all our venial sins and helps us to ward off mortal sins.

The strength of the spirit also redounds to the benefit of the body. Only the most hardened materialist would deny that the maladies of the soul affect the health of the body. Guilt, shame, anxiety, anger, envy, laziness, lust — these spiritual ills, left unchecked, inevitably work themselves out in bodily breakdowns.

The Eucharist is the "medicine of immortality," as one ancient father called it. The sacrament heals us, body and soul, and prepares us for the life we will lead in eternity. What is not healed now will be fully restored at the resurrection of the body.

Do not hesitate to ask the Lord to heal you. Do not doubt for a moment that you will one day be healed.

✠

24. He Gives Himself

To them he gave . . .
His very flesh, his very blood.

In the original Latin of the "Verbum Supernum," St. Thomas makes clear what attribute unites his themes of Trinity, Incarnation, and Eucharist. It is the self-giving love of charity.

In stanza two he writes that Jesus *gave himself* to his disciples as food. In stanza three, he adds: *He gave them* "his very flesh, his very blood." Stanza four tells the story of Jesus' earthly life in a kind of litany of self-donation. Literally translated the passage would read: "When he was born *he gave himself* to us as a companion; while at table *he gave himself* to be our food; dying *he gave himself* as our ransom; now reigning *he gives himself* as our reward."

This love that Jesus showed to mankind is the overflow of the inner life of the Trinity. The inner life of the Trinity is charity, complete self-giving love of one Person for another.

Jesus gave himself completely. He held nothing back, not even his life. To this love he calls us, now, to learn from him and to live toward one another.

The Eucharist is the key. Thomas said: "The Eucharist is the sacrament which expresses Christ's love — and causes our love."

This sacrament gives us abundant grace — which is our share in the divine life — to practice the virtue of charity. St. John of Damascus compared the Eucharist to the burning coal that Isaiah saw (Is 6:6): "For a live ember is not simply wood, but wood united to fire; so also the bread of Communion is not simple bread, but bread united with the Godhead."

And like a live coal, God's charity gives us heat, light, and energy enough to share. In the words of Gregory the Great: "God's love is never idle; for, wherever it is, it does great works." The love of Christ presses us onward (2 Cor 5:14).

We will not possess ourselves until, like Christ, we have given ourselves away.

☩

25. Companion

By birth our fellow man was he.

In becoming man, God became our *socius* — our companion, ally, partner, fellow — our friend. God has visited his people, not as a stranger, not as a conquering invader, but as an intimate — a man like us, in all things but sin. "He had to be made like his brethren in every respect. . . . For because he himself has suffered and been tempted, he is able to help those who are tempted" (Heb 2:17-18).

This closeness frightens many people. Any human intimacy can be daunting. Friendship makes demands. It requires time, commitment, conversation, a sharing of goods, the opening of one's heart. It leaves us vulnerable to betrayal. It left Jesus vulnerable to betrayal!

The cost of friendship is high, and many people today would rather not pay the price — not for a human, and certainly not for God, who can be notoriously demanding of his friends. We would prefer, perhaps, to keep our God at a reverent and safe distance.

But this is not an option. Jesus said to his apostles: "No longer do I call you servants . . . but I have called you friends" (Jn 15:15). With those words, he closed the gap between God and us, and he sealed it tight. He pronounced those words at the Last Supper, when he instituted the Eucharist.

The Eucharist is the sacrament of friendship. "It is the special feature of friendship to live together with friends," said Thomas. "Christ promises us as a reward that we shall live in heaven in his bodily presence. But even in our earthly pilgrimage he does not deprive us of his bodily presence, but unites us with himself in this sacrament through the truth of his body and blood."

The Eucharist is the sacrament of friendship; it is the sacrament of charity. In the *Summa*, St. Thomas uses those words almost interchangeably: "charity is friendship."

Christ's friendship will press us on to friendship with others, even difficult people, because Christ has befriended them first, and we want to share his friendship. "So much do we love our friends," said Thomas, "that for their sake we love all who belong to them, even if they hurt or hate us. The friendship of charity extends even to our enemies, whom we love out of charity in relation to God, to whom the friendship of charity is chiefly directed."

"Charity, which above all is friendship . . . extends to sinners, whom, out of charity, we love for God's sake."

Our friendship with Christ does not preclude deep reverence toward him. Quite the contrary is true. Throughout the Corpus Christi poems, Thomas artfully alternates the language of friendship and brotherhood with the reverential language of the Mass.

The closer we draw, the more awesome we know him to be. He is most awesome when he is inches away in the tabernacle or within us in Holy Communion.

☩

26. Victim

O saving Victim, opening wide
The gate of heaven to man below . . .
Thine aid supply, thy strength bestow.

In this day and age, we are baffled by the idea of sacrifice. We grimace when we read of the rivers of blood that flowed from the offerings in the Temple in Jerusalem.

But religion has always demanded sacrifice. Indeed, the very word *religion* — from the Latin word meaning "to bind" — implies a relinquishing of freedom. We give up what is ours, acknowledging that it all belongs to someone greater. What we offer in sacrifice we call the "victim" or the "host."

St. Thomas tells us three reasons why we must offer sacrifice. We make our offerings, first of all, for the remission of sin (Heb 5:1), by which we are turned away from God. Second, we sacrifice so that we may be preserved in a state of grace, by ever adhering to God, the source of peace and salvation. Thus, under the old Law, the sacrifice of peace-offerings was offered for the salvation of those making the offering (Lev 3). Finally, we offer sacrifice so that our spirit will be perfectly united to God — a union that will be most perfectly realized in glory. Thus, under the old Law, priests offered a holocaust — so called because the victim was *wholly* burnt (Lev 1).

Yet no animal victim could make up for the sins of humanity; for even the smallest sin takes on infinite proportions when we consider that it is an offense against almighty God. No creature, offered in holocaust, could make restitution for humanity's rebellion; no burnt offering could reconcile us to God. To make up for an offense of infinite proportion, we would need to offer a victim equally infinite.

Mankind satisfies this condition only in the humanity of Jesus Christ. For, through him, our sins were blotted out (Rom 4:25); through him we received the grace of salvation (Heb 5:9); through him we have acquired the perfection of glory (Heb 10:19). Christ himself, as man, was not only priest, but also a perfect victim, a victim for sin, for a peace-offering, and a holocaust.

Both priest and victim, Christ did not kill himself, but of his own free will he exposed himself to death. For our sake, he freely gave himself over to suffering.

Today, he manifests himself as priest and victim in the sacrifice of the Mass. In the Mass — which is our participation in the once-for-all sacrifice of the cross — he satisfies the demands of religion, which we could never satisfy. As lamb of God, he takes away the sins of the world.

Let us, every day, join many small sacrifices to his unique sacrifice, till the day when he, who was lifted up on the cross — and is lifted up in the Mass — has drawn all the world to himself (Jn 12:32).

☩

27. Spiritual Warfare

Our foes press on from every side;
Thine aid supply, thy strength bestow.

"The life of man upon earth," said St. Thomas, quoting the Latin Bible, "is warfare" (Jb 7:1).

We are at war within ourselves first of all. "I see in my members another law at war with the law of my mind and making me captive to the law of sin" (Rom 7:23). Though we see that virtue is reasonable and sin is not, we give in to temptation and sin anyway.

We are at war with ourselves, but also with something much more powerful than we are. The demons are ever assailing us: "Your adversary the devil prowls around like a roaring lion, seeking someone to devour" (1 Pt 5:8). The demons envy us because of our hope of salvation in Jesus Christ, and so they attack us by instigating us to sin. As Christ wills our eternal life, the demons wish our spiritual death.

The demons wield mighty intellectual powers. They are fallen angels who have chosen not to serve God. As spirits, they can insinuate themselves into our thoughts and exercise a powerful, persuasive influence on our minds and actions. They can also simulate miracles and manipulate the material world in spectacular ways.

So the contest between man and demon is not waged on a level playing field. But God has more than made up for our deficiencies. For he gives us grace enough to overcome all the devil's weaponry. "My grace is sufficient for you," he told St. Paul, "for my power is made perfect in weakness" (2 Cor 12:9). Indeed, God sometimes permits the devils to assault us because, by resisting them, we grow stronger. At other times, when we have neglected the Lord, he permits the demons to prevail over us, or cause us pain, so that we will turn to him again in our need.

The preeminent source of grace is the Holy Eucharist. If we receive Christ regularly and adore him in the sacrament, we can enter battle with the assurance of victory.

We also enjoy the protection of the angels who have remained true to God. Everyone has a guardian angel appointed by God. These angels work out God's providence on earth, and they are more powerful than any demons. Thus we can echo the prophet Elijah as he entered the field of battle: "Fear not, for those who are with us are more than those who are with them" (2 Kgs 6:16).

Since the earliest days of the Church, Christians devoted to the Eucharist have also shown a deep devotion to the angels. Where the King reigns, the angels surround his throne. When we pray before the Lord in the Blessed Sacrament, we pray in the midst of countless angels of heaven.

Call upon them. They will surely defend you in battle.

✛

✝

28. Our True Native Land

O grant us endless length of days
In our true native land with thee.

As long as we live in this state of life, we are pilgrims on the road, journeying toward heaven. The moment we were "born again" in baptism, we were no longer natives of the land of our birth. We became exiles from heaven.

By grace, we live with a longing for our homeland, our *patria*. Though we try to satisfy this longing with other things, nothing suffices. All earthly pleasures ultimately fail us. Age takes away our taste for favorite foods. On a certain day, the stairway in our dream home becomes too steep for us to climb. Death divides friend from friend, parents from children, lover from beloved, husband from wife.

God has designed nature to prepare us well for heaven. Aging detaches us from the things of this world, so that nothing should weigh us down on our journey. We should return to God like refugees who have abandoned everything but the desire to see our home.

St. Thomas uses these images everywhere to describe our life on earth. We are wayfarers. We are pilgrims. We live in hope that we will reach our destination, certain that our Father God will give us all we need to get there.

In this context, Thomas recalls the angel's words to the prophet Elijah: "Arise and eat, else the journey will be too great for you." Elijah got up and ate and drank, and "went in the strength of that food forty days and forty nights to Horeb the mount of God" (1 Kgs 19:7-8). The food and drink, of course, are types of the Eucharist; Mount Horeb is a foreshadowing of heaven.

Thomas Aquinas was literally a wayfarer when his final illness struck. He asked his companions to carry him to a wayside monastery. Arriving at the door, he could barely stand; "he clung with his hand to the doorpost." He knew he was on the last mile of his journey. He wanted to see Jesus.

When the monks brought him the sacrament, the friar — though feeble with illness — dropped to his knees to greet his Savior and friend.

He was almost home. Perhaps we are, too. We know neither the day nor the hour. Our time may be short — we'll never know — but we should have a clearer notion of the distance we need to cover and the baggage that weighs us down.

In the presence of Our Lord, let us examine ourselves, asking what we need to do in order to move ahead, and what we need to let go. We cannot rise to God if we are attached to the earth.

✠

V. *Adoro Te Devote*

Godhead Here in Hiding

Adoro Te Devote

Adoro te devote, latens Deitas,
Quae sub his figuris vere latitas:
Tibi se cor meum totum subiicit,
Quia te contemplans totum deficit.

Visus, tactus, gustus in te fallitur,
Sed auditu solo tuto creditur.
Credo quidquid dixit Dei Filius:
Nil hoc verbo Veritatis verius.

In cruce latebat sola Deitas,
At hic latet simul et humanitas;
Ambo tamen credens atque confitens,
Peto quod petivit latro paenitens.

Plagas, sicut Thomas, non intueor;
Deum tamen meum te confiteor.
Fac me tibi semper magis credere,
In te spem habere, te diligere.

O memoriale mortis Domini!
Panis vivus, vitam praestans homini!
Praesta meae menti de te vivere
Et te illi semper dulce sapere.

Godhead Here in Hiding

Godhead here in hiding, whom I do adore
Masked by these bare shadows, shape and nothing
    more,
See, Lord, at thy service low lies here a heart
Lost, all lost in wonder at the God thou art.

Seeing, touching, tasting are in thee deceived;
How says trusty hearing? That shall be believed:
What God's Son has told me, take for truth I do;
Truth himself speaks truly or there's nothing true.

On the cross thy Godhead made no sign to men;
Here thy very manhood steals from human ken:
Both are my confession, both are my belief,
And I pray the prayer of the dying thief.

I am not like Thomas, wounds I cannot see,
But can plainly call thee Lord and God as he:
This faith each day deeper be my holding of,
Daily make me harder hope and dearer love.

O thou our reminder of Christ crucified,
Living bread the life of us for whom he died,
Lend this life to me then: feed and feast my mind,
There be thou the sweetness man was meant to
    find.

Pie pellicane, Iesu Domine,
Me immundum munda tuo sanguine;
Cuius una stilla salvum facere
Totum mundum quit ab omni scelere.

Iesu, quem velatum nunc aspicio,
Oro fiat illud quod tam sitio;
Ut te revelata cernens facie,
Visu sim beatus tuae gloriae.

Bring the tender tale true of the Pelican;
Bathe me, Jesu Lord, in what thy bosom ran —
Blood that but one drop of has the worth to win
All the world forgiveness of its world of sin.

Jesu whom I look at shrouded here below,
I beseech thee send me what I thirst for so,
Some day to gaze on thee face to face in light
And be blest for ever with thy glory's sight.

— TRANSLATION BY GERARD MANLEY HOPKINS

✠

29. Veils and Shadows

Godhead here in hiding, whom I do adore
Masked by these bare shadows, shape and nothing more.

Thomas often spoke of the appearances of bread and wine as "veils" of the Blessed Sacrament. "Our bodily eye, on account of the sacramental species, is hindered from beholding the body of Christ underlying them . . . just as we are hindered from seeing what is covered with any corporeal veil."

The poet T.S. Eliot wrote that humankind cannot bear very much reality. There's much truth to that. For survival's sake, for sanity's sake, we must limit the things to which we give our attention, in which we invest our emotion. Pains and pleasures abound in the world. We cannot bear to contemplate them all.

Nor can we begin to contemplate the abyss of suffering and joy that hides behind the sacramental signs of the Eucharist. God gave us the appearances of bread and wine as if to put a shade on a lamp that would otherwise dazzle our eyes.

Thus shaded, the sacrament casts light by which we can see more and more of what is real. We *can* bear more reality, as we behold it in the light of Christ — as we bear it with the help of Christ.

The great Dominican scholar Gerald Vann wrote: "If we are to see the truth in its entirety we must be prepared to say *adoro devote*; and because we are not prepared, we miss the truth."

Let us resolve to spend more time before this light, the light of the world (Jn 9:5). Here, in the light God has kindly adjusted to our eyes, we may see things as they are.

30. The Heart

See, Lord, at thy service low lies here a heart . . .

You could fill a small library with books on the mind of St. Thomas — books that would show little of his heart. We revere him as the Angelic Doctor, and rightly, but it is possible to overemphasize his intellect.

Thomas had a will and a heart, both eloquent and evident in the affection he shows in his poetry and prayer. We have seen that he ordinarily shed tears at Holy Communion, and that he leaned his head in love upon the tabernacle when he was troubled.

Affection, however, does not — or at least should not — depend exclusively upon our emotions. Thomas's emotions, like our own, surely knew ups and downs. Yet he was consistent in his affection.

Human love is like a fire that, at first, blazes wildly as the tinder catches. When the flames settle down to embers, the fire requires much more care so that it does not die out but continues to radiate warmth.

When a relationship is new, affection arises spontaneously in the heart. Every day we are moved by fresh discoveries about our beloved. But, over time, loving affection proves more a matter of the will than the emotions. We *choose* to show our love, even if we are not feeling especially affectionate. For, if familiarity does not necessarily breed contempt, it does often foster neglect and a certain coldness. We can grow so familiar with someone that we lose interest and seek novelties — hobbies, distractions, pastimes.

We need to tend love's fires with constancy. This is as true in our dealings with God as it is in our life with a spouse. We need to remain constant in conversational prayer, and we should rely on certain short, set phrases that express our love — as Thomas prayed the same small prayer at the consecration of the Mass every day.

Thomas left us his prayer for a steadfast heart; and we can make it our own:

> *Give me, O Lord, a steadfast heart,*
> *which no unworthy affection may drag downwards;*
> *give me an unconquered heart, which no tribulation can*
> *   wear out;*
> *give me an upright heart, which no unworthy purpose*
> *   may tempt aside.*
> *Bestow on me also, O Lord my God,*
> *understanding to know you,*
> *wisdom to find you,*
> *and a faithfulness that may finally embrace you,*
> *through Jesus Christ Our Lord. Amen.*

31. Lost in Wonder

Lost, all lost in wonder at the God thou art.

Prolific, productive, prodigious — pick your adjective. St. Thomas wrote his first major work at age twenty-two. Many other works followed, one after another, year after year. He wrote to strengthen faith, to shore up morals, to reconcile secular philosophers with churchmen, to unite the separated Eastern and Western churches. He wrote a comprehensive manual for missionaries. And in his enormous *Summa Theologica*, he conceived, in the words of one biographer, "a luminous summary, which should contain the whole of Christianity from the existence of God to the least precept of morality."

By the time he set to work on the *Summa*, he was in his mid-forties, and he was already renowned as the greatest living theologian. But those who read portions of this new work-in-progress recognized it as more than the masterpiece of a genius. It was an historic event.

The *Summa* consumed Thomas's attention. During a three-year period, he produced more than a thousand words of finished, polished prose per day. He dictated to four secretaries simultaneously, on four different subjects. While one was catching up with his thought, he'd turn to another, then another, then another. His colleagues claimed that he dictated in his sleep.

He poured himself into this great theological labor. And he prayed as hard as he worked, taking each topic before the Lord long before he considered putting his thoughts to paper.

One morning, though, while Thomas was saying Mass, something momentous happened. He never said what he had experienced — but afterward he "refused to write or dictate; indeed he put away his writing materials." His chief secretary was baffled. He feared that overwork had made Thomas a little crazy. He begged his master to continue the *Summa*. But Thomas only answered him: "Reginald, I cannot — because all that I have written seems to me so much straw. . . . All that I have written seems to me like straw compared with what has now been revealed to me."

The brightest lanterns, though helpful by night, are superfluous in the daylight. We put them aside. Beyond the mighty shadows is a far greater Reality — which casts all the shadows.

At the pinnacle of theology is a vision of God that surpasses all theology.

Thus Thomas's work ended, not with a last word, but with a burst of light too brilliant for us to see — though we may be gazing into it now. Though the *Summa* was left unfinished, it found a fitting completion.

Though Thomas knew much about the world, he never grew cynical. He never lost his capacity for wonder. With innocent eyes, he saw things as God created them to be, in their essence.

Let us take for ourselves the blind beggar's prayer: Lord, that I, too, may see! (Mk 10:51).

32. The Sweetness

Lend this life to me then: feed and feast my mind,
There be thou the sweetness man was meant to find.

The grace we receive in Holy Communion comes to its full maturity only in heaven. But our hoped-for heavenly reward does not prevent all rewards during our life on earth. The Blessed Sacrament has its sensible rewards, even here and now.

For Holy Communion gives us more than just an increase in grace. It gives us also, said St. Thomas, a certain taste of spiritual sweetness. The soul is spiritually gladdened, as if it were drunk with the sweet taste of divine goodness. "Eat, O friends, and drink; drink deeply, O lovers" (Sg 5:1).

St. Paul said that Christ is a "fragrant offering" (Eph 5:2). And even King Solomon foretasted this sacramental sweetness when he spoke of the "food of angels . . . providing every pleasure and suited to every taste. For thy sustenance manifested thy sweetness toward thy children; and the bread, ministering to the desire of the one who took it, was changed to suit everyone's liking" (Wis 16:20-21).

The Lord delights in your purest delights. He knows your desires, and he himself has "earnestly desired to eat this Passover with you" (Lk 22:15). A gracious and hospitable host, he will surely serve your spirit what is most to its taste.

We cannot, however, enjoy his spiritual sweetness without first preparing ourselves for it. Nor could we enjoy any earthly banquet without first preparing ourselves. If we arrive at the table after glutting ourselves on junk food and overbearing flavors, we cannot enjoy the delicacies put before us. In the same way, we lose our taste for spiritual sweetness if we approach the Lord's table with a mind distracted through venial sins.

Through our penance, our fasts, and our prayer, may we prepare ourselves well for our next Communion. He has given us bread from heaven, having all sweetness within it.

☩

33. The Pelican

Bring the tender tale true of the Pelican;
Bathe me, Jesu Lord, in what thy bosom ran —
Blood that but one drop of has the worth to win
All the world forgiveness of its world of sin.

To be deeply Catholic is to see Christ in everything. St. Thomas saw types of salvation everywhere in the Old Testament. And pious Christians have always sought signs of Christ in creation as well. Mariners, for example, observed the dolphin bearing ship-wrecked men to the surface of the sea, and they saw it as a fitting symbol of Christ, who lifts sinners up from the depths and guides them to safe harbor.

In a similar way, the pelican became an ancient symbol of Jesus in the Eucharist. Devout Christians observed that the mother pelican pecked at her breast before feeding her young. They concluded that, with her beak, she was drawing blood from her heart to sustain her hatchlings. The mother pelican's seeming self-sacrifice reminded believers of their Lord, who even now feeds the Church with his own flesh and blood.

Our Catholic ancestors were wrong about the pelican. She wasn't piercing her breast or drawing blood from her heart; she was catching live insects. But they were right about Christ, who feeds us from his own substance.

The great poet Gerard Manley Hopkins gives his translation a contemporary twist: *Bring the tender tale true of the Pelican*. A modern man with a modicum of zoology may know that the ancients were wrong about the seabird's feeding habits. But a modern Christian — even a zoologist — can still pray for the fulfillment of the ancient metaphor.

Bathe me, Jesu Lord, in what thy bosom ran.

34. Thomas

I am not like Thomas, wounds I cannot see,
But can plainly call thee Lord and God as he.

St. Thomas draws a smile here as he invokes his apostolic namesake. Thomas protests that he is unlike Thomas.

The apostle Thomas refused to believe Jesus had risen until he had seen him and probed the wounds in his hands and side (Jn 20:24ff).

Surely Thomas shared some traits with the apostle. Thomas Aquinas esteemed sensory evidence no less than the apostle, and he was just as exacting in his insistence that the mysteries must not contradict reason. But Thomas Aquinas grasped something that his patron did not.

Faith is, by definition, "the assurance of things hoped for, the conviction of things *not seen*" (Heb 11:1; emphasis added). Indeed, appearances can be deceiving. "No one should doubt concerning the faith," Thomas preached in a homily. "Rather, he ought to believe things pertinent to faith *more* than what he sees. For man's sight can be deceived, but God's knowledge is never mistaken."

St. Paul said faith comes by hearing (Rom 10:17), and Aquinas, in the "Adoro Te Devote," echoes this:

Seeing, touching, tasting are in thee deceived;
How says trusty hearing? That shall be believed.

It's not that the human auditory sense ranks above the visual. It is, rather, that hearing — in Paul's sense of the word — implies an act of trust. We hear; we listen; we accept what we hear, because the speaker speaks with authority.

What God's Son has told me, take for truth I do;
Truth himself speaks truly or there's nothing true.

The voice of Christ, and of his Church, conveys something that surpasses the power of the natural human senses — it conveys "things not seen." The mysteries of Christ require supernatural faith.

Thomas once preached: "Someone may say: 'Isn't it stupid to believe what is not seen; shouldn't we refuse to believe things that are not seen?' "

He went on to answer his own question: "If man could know perfectly all things visible and invisible, it *would* be stupid to believe what we do not see. However, our knowledge is so imperfect that no philosopher has ever been able to make a perfect investigation of the nature of a single fly. . . . If our intellect is so feeble, then, isn't it stupid to *refuse* to believe anything about God, other than what man can know by himself? . . . 'Behold God is great, exceeding our knowledge' (Jb 36:26)."

✠

35. Face to Face

Jesu whom I look at shrouded here below,
I beseech thee send me what I thirst for so,
Some day to gaze on thee face to face in light
And be blest for ever with thy glory's sight.

This final stanza of St. Thomas's poetry echoes the prayer he made before Communion every day: "Most loving Father, grant that your beloved Son, whom I now receive veiled, I may one day behold face to face forever."

Thomas longed to see the face of Christ. Can we say the same of ourselves?

Knowing our own weakness, can we bear to face up to Jesus' loving demands?

Knowing how faithful he has been to us — how he has kept us in his heart from all eternity — and how little we have given him in return — do we dare to lift our eyes to his?

St. Peter sized up the situation perfectly when he fell to Jesus' feet and said, "Depart from me, for I am a sinful man, O Lord" (Lk 5:8).

But Jesus lifted Peter up with the words, "Do not be afraid" (v. 10). Neither should we be afraid to gaze upon him. For it is he who lifts us up from our shame and humiliation.

By grace, we rise again and again to look upon a love we could never deserve, could never return in full.

Jesus wants us to look at him, to worship him in the Holy Eucharist. His Real Presence now will prepare us for the fullness of vision, a Communion that never ends, in our true native land — in heaven.

Christ will have no more glory on the day we arrive in heaven than he does in the moments when we gaze upon him in the tabernacle or the monstrance. For his glories are eternal and unchanging. The difference on that day will be entirely ours. "We shall be like him, for we shall see him as he is" (1 Jn 3:2) — face to face.

May our every moment in the presence of Our Lord, and in Communion with Our Lord, be as loving and as reverent as if it were our last. One day it will be.

✠

Appendix

Prayer Before Communion
by St. Thomas Aquinas

Almighty and ever-living God, I approach the sacrament of your only begotten Son, Our Lord Jesus Christ. I come sick to the doctor of life, unclean to the fountain of mercy, blind to the radiance of eternal light, and poor and needy to the Lord of heaven and earth.

Lord, in your great generosity, heal my sickness, wash away my defilement, enlighten my blindness, enrich my poverty, and clothe my nakedness. May I receive the bread of angels, the King of Kings and Lord of Lords, with humble reverence, with the purity and faith, the repentance and love, and the determined purpose that will help to bring me to salvation. May I receive the sacrament of the Lord's body and blood and its reality and power.

Kind God, may I receive the body of your only begotten Son, Our Lord Jesus Christ, born from the womb of the Virgin Mary, and so be received into his mystical body and numbered among his members.

Loving Father, as on my earthly pilgrimage I now receive your beloved Son under the veil of a sacrament, may I one day see him face to face in glory, who lives and reigns with you forever. Amen.

Prayer After Communion
by St. Thomas Aquinas

Lord, Father, all-powerful and ever-living God, I thank you, for even though I am a sinner, your unprofitable servant, not because of my worth but in the kindness of your mercy, you have fed me with the precious body and blood of your Son, Our Lord Jesus Christ. I pray that this Holy Communion may bring me not condemnation and punishment, but forgiveness and salvation. May it be a helmet of faith and a shield of good will. May it purify me from evil ways and put an end to my evil passions. May it bring me charity and patience, humility and obedience, and growth in the power to do good. May it be my strong defense against all my enemies, visible and invisible, and the perfect calming of all my evil impulses, bodily and spiritual. May it unite me more closely to you, the one true God, and lead me safely through death to everlasting happiness with you. And I pray that you will lead me, a sinner, to the banquet where you, with your Son and Holy Spirit, are true and perfect light, total fulfillment, everlasting joy, gladness without end, and perfect happiness to your saints. Grant this through Christ Our Lord. Amen.

Sources

Baring-Gould, Sabine. 1897. *Lives of the Saints*. London: John Nimmo.

Bourke, Vernon J., ed. 1960. *The Pocket Aquinas*. New York: Washington Square Press.

Britt, Dom Matthew, O.S.B. 1952. *The Hymns of the Breviary and Missal*. New York: Benziger Brothers.

Bunson, Matthew. 1994. *The Angelic Doctor: The Life and World of St. Thomas Aquinas*. Huntington, Ind.: Our Sunday Visitor.

Chesterton, G.K. 1933. *Saint Thomas Aquinas: The Dumb Ox*. New York: Doubleday (1956 reprint).

Chenu, M.D., O.P. 1964. *Toward Understanding St. Thomas*. Chicago: Henry Regnery.

Clark, Mary T., ed. 1972. *An Aquinas Reader*. New York: Doubleday Image.

Coffey, Reginald M., O.P. 1944. *The Man from Rocca Sicca*. Milwaukee: Bruce Publishing.

Crashaw, Richard. 1949. *The Verse in English of Richard Crashaw*. New York: Grove Press.

D'Arcy, Martin C., S.J. 1954. *St. Thomas Aquinas*. Westminster, Md.: The Newman Press.

Foster, Kenelm, O.P. 1959. *The Life of St. Thomas Aquinas: Biographical Documents*. London: Longmans, Green.

Gilson, Etienne. 1929. *The Philosophy of St. Thomas Aquinas*. New York: Dorset (reprint).

Grabmann, Martin. 1951. *The Interior Life of St. Thomas Aquinas*. Milwaukee: Bruce Publishing.

Henry, H.T. 1912. *Eucharistica: Verse and Prose in Honor of the Hidden God*. Philadelphia: The Dolphin Press.

Hopkins, Gerard M., S.J. 1967. *The Poems of Gerard Manley Hopkins*. Edited by W.H. Gardner and N.H. MacKenzie. London: Oxford.

Maritain, Jacques. 1958. *St. Thomas Aquinas*. New York: Meridian.

Maritain, Raissa. 1955. *The Angel of the Schools*. New York: Sheed and Ward.

Maynard, Theodore. 1955. *Saints for Our Times*. New York: Doubleday Image.

Messenger, Ruth Ellis. 1953. *The Medieval Latin Hymn*. Washington: Capital Press.

Neale, J.M. 1863. *Medieval Hymns and Sequences*. London: Joseph Masters.

Pieper, Josef. 1987. *Guide to Thomas Aquinas*. Notre Dame, Ind.: University of Notre Dame Press.

Raby, F.J.E. 1953. *A History of Christian-Latin Poetry*. London: Oxford University Press.

Raby, F.J.E. 1957. *Poetry of the Eucharist*. London: A.R. Mowbray.

Schaff, Philip. 1870. *Christ in Song*. London: Sampson Low, Son, and Marston.

Sertillanges, A.G., O.P. 1933. *Saint Thomas Aquinas and His Work*. London: Burns, Oates and Washbourne.

Socias, James, ed. 1995. *Handbook of Prayers*. Huntington, Ind.: Our Sunday Visitor.

Sullivan, Mark. 1993. "Comparing Aquinas's 'Lauda, Sion' with Question 75 of the Third Part of the *Summa*." Unpublished paper.

Thomas Aquinas. 1993. *Devoutly I Adore Thee: The Prayers and Hymns of St. Thomas Aquinas*. Manchester, N.H.: Sophia Institute Press.

Thomas Aquinas. [1947 edition.] *Summa Theologica*. New York: Benziger Brothers.

Vandeur, Eugene, O.S.B. 1939. *Adoro Te: Contemplation of the Most Holy Eucharist*. New York: Benziger Brothers.

Vann, Gerald, O.P. 1947. *St. Thomas Aquinas*. New York: Benziger Brothers.

Waddell, Helen. 1977. *More Latin Lyrics, from Virgil to Milton*. New York: Norton.

Zawilla, Ronald John, O.P. 1985. *The Historiae Corporis Christi Attributed to Thomas Aquinas: A Theological Study of Their Biblical Sources*. Doctoral dissertation, University of Toronto.

Zundel, Veronica. 1984. *Eerdmans' Book of Famous Prayers*. Grand Rapids, Mich.: Eerdmans.

Our Sunday Visitor . . .
Your Source for Discovering the Riches of the Catholic Faith

Our Sunday Visitor has an extensive line of materials for young children, teens, and adults. Our books, Bibles, booklets, CD-ROMs, audios, and videos are available in bookstores worldwide.

To receive a FREE full-line catalog or for more information, call **Our Sunday Visitor** at **1–800–348–2440**. Or write, **Our Sunday Visitor** / 200 Noll Plaza / Huntington, IN 46750.

- -

Please send me: __A catalog
Please send me materials on:
__Apologetics and catechetics __Reference works
__Prayer books   __Heritage and the saints
__The family   __The parish
Name_____
Address_____Apt._____
City_____State____Zip_____
Telephone (   ) _____

A23BBABP

- -

Please send a friend: __A catalog
Please send a friend materials on:
__Apologetics and catechetics __Reference works
__Prayer books   __Heritage and the saints
__The family   __The parish
Name_____
Address_____Apt._____
City_____State____Zip_____
Telephone (   ) _____

A23BBABP

- -

Our Sunday Visitor
200 Noll Plaza
Huntington, IN 46750
Toll free: **1–800–348–2440**
E-mail: osvbooks@osv.com
Website: www.osv.com